Prices, Markets,

and the

Pharmaceutical

Revolution

John E. Calfee

The AEI Press

Publisher for the American Enterprise Institute

WASHINGTON, D.C.

2000

Available in the United States from the AEI Press, c/o Publisher Resources Inc., 1224 Heil Quaker Blvd., P.O. Box 7001, La Vergne, TN 37086-7001. Distributed outside the United States by arrangement with Eurospan, 3 Henrietta Street, London WC2E 8LU England.

ISBN 0-8447-7147-3

The AEI Press
Publisher for the American Enterprise Institute
1150 17th Street, N.W., Washington, D.C. 20036

Printed in the United States of America

Contents

Acknowledgments

The author wishes to acknowledge the research assistance of Tericke Blanchard and Randolph Stempski of the American Enterprise Institute and the helpful comments of Christopher DeMuth, Robert Helms, Alison Keith, Mark McClellan, and Sam Peltzman on earlier drafts. I am, of course, responsible for any errors.

1
Introduction

Pharmaceutical costs have aroused controversy for decades, but debate has intensified over the past year. Discussions have pursued several themes.[1] One is the rapid increase in the expenditures for pharmaceuticals and the prices of some drugs. Another is the delineation and condemnation of price differences between the United States and other nations (especially Canada and Mexico) and among various domestic buyers, including the federal government, managed care organizations, and pharmacies that cater to individual consumers. Discussions frequently target the promotion of pharmaceuticals (especially when directed at consumers), which is blamed for high prices, excessive expenditures, and inappropriate medication. Industry taxes have come under scrutiny for being too low, and profits, for being too high. Finally, there has been much talk of whether and how to end the seemingly anomalous omission of drug benefits from Medicare, which covers virtually all other important medical products and services for the elderly.

Price controls—to be achieved by design or by implication—have become a political issue. Numerous federal and state legislators have proposed reducing pharmaceutical prices by various methods such as extending Medicaid discounts to neighborhood pharmacies, cutting U.S. prices to match those charged in Canada and Mexico, and even implementing direct controls.[2] President William Clinton and other political leaders, along with interested organizations and advocacy groups, have proposed adding a drug benefit to the Medicare program, often with special mechanisms for negotiating drug prices.[3] Although no legislation has passed so far, there is every reason to believe that pharmaceutical prices and reimbursement will be an enduring political issue. Indeed, officials in the Clinton administration have observed that price controls on pharmaceuticals could be inevitable, absent substantial changes in industry behavior.[4]

The impulse to address pharmaceutical prices through political means is deeply misconceived and could thwart today's dramatic, but still incipient, advances in biological science and medical practice. These concerns go well beyond the economist's usual abhorrence of price controls and government allocation of resources. As detailed later in this essay, the recent attacks on pharmaceutical prices and expenditures betray an ignorance of the fundamental changes underway in pharmaceutical research, development, and marketing. The dramatic increases in spending on pharmaceuticals are a natural and desirable reflection of two forms of progress: *scientific* advances in pharmaceutical research and biotechnology and *institutional* advances in drug testing, information processing, and the dissemination of knowledge among scientists, manufacturers, doctors, patients, consumers, and managed care organizations.

Those advances in pharmaceutical research and development have expanded the scope of drug treatment by providing superior new treatments to existing patients and offering many previously untreated consumers new opportunities to improve their health. The expanded boundaries of drug therapy have other equally important consequences, including a need for more information among consumers and physicians—which advertising and promotion can partly provide—and the addition of new elements of risk to the research environment. Finally, the fact that the current revolution in research is in the early stages prevents knowing the value of the next generation of new pharmaceuticals or what consumers will want to spend on drug therapy. Because the revolution involves not only rapidly advancing science but rapidly evolving institutions and markets, the potential damage from price or spending controls over pharmaceuticals is even greater than from controls over stable commodities such as petroleum products and residential apartments.

The implications for the politics of health are clear. Price controls would be exceptionally dangerous as a disincentive to further research in developing new drugs as well as in finding better ways to use existing drugs. Dismantling such controls would be difficult. Spending caps could deprive consumers of much value from new drug therapies. Congress must exercise extreme caution in adding a Medicare benefit for prescription drugs so as to avoid the error of depriving patients of future benefits that would far exceed their costs.

2

Why Everyone Is Spending More on Pharmaceuticals

The Worldwide Increase in Pharmaceutical Expenditures

Pharmaceutical expenditures have been increasing rapidly. Figure 1 shows that outpatient expenditures on prescription drugs (with inflation taken into account) almost doubled between 1990 and 1998. The increases have been larger in recent years, with the largest (12.3 percent) in 1998.[5] Pharmaceuticals are also claiming an increasing share of the U.S. health care budget. Some historical perspective is useful here. Prescription costs as a proportion of health care expenditures actually declined for many years after 1960, with the trend reversing in the early 1980s. Even today, the share of spending on pharmaceuticals is still far below the levels of the early 1960s, although it has climbed from 4.9 percent of health care costs in 1985 to 7.2 percent in 1997 (see figure 2).

FIGURE 1

REAL EXPENDITURES ON PRESCRIPTION DRUGS IN THE UNITED
STATES, 1990–1998

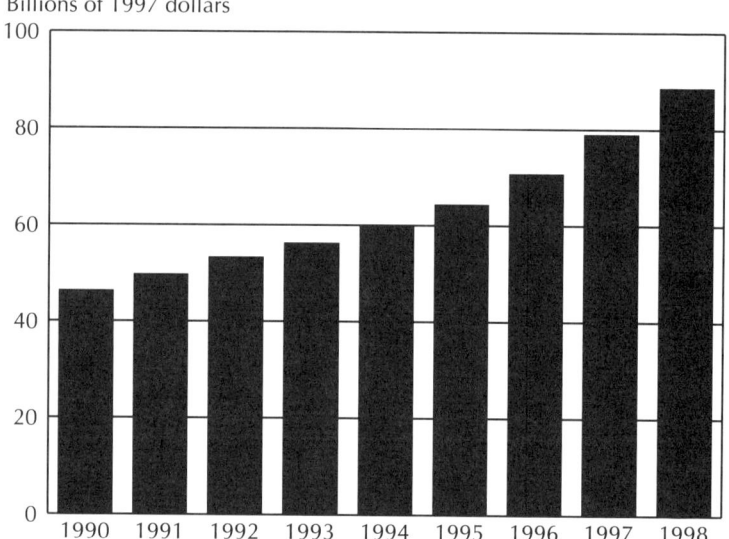

NOTE: Expenditures have been deflated by the CPI-U.
SOURCE: HCFA 1999.

Most forecasters see pharmaceutical expenditures continuing to increase at 10 percent or more annually. The Health Care Financing Administration (HCFA), for example, estimates that prescription drug costs increased by 13 percent in 1999 and will continue to grow, though at a rate that will decline gradually from 11 percent in 2000 to 9 percent in 2008.[6]

Other advanced economies have also seen rapid increases in pharmaceutical expenditures—worldwide retail pharmacy purchases increased by 9 percent between September 1998 and September 1999—and these nations expect continuing increases,[7] despite the fact that the pro-

John E. Calfee

FIGURE 2
PRESCRIPTION DRUGS AS A PERCENTAGE OF U.S. NATIONAL
HEALTH EXPENDITURES, 1960–1997

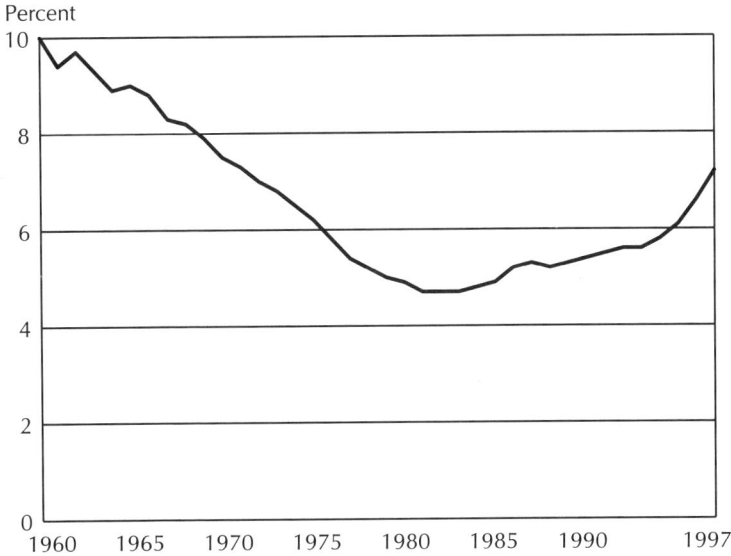

SOURCE: HCFA 1999, table 2.

portion of health care expenditures devoted to pharmaceuticals in many westernized economies is already far
larger than in the United States. Figure 3 indicates that the
7 percent allocation of health care costs in the United
States today is barely half of the corresponding amount in
Canada or Germany and even further below the levels in
Japan, the United Kingdom, and France.[8]

Price increases are not the main reason for increased
drug expenditures. Since 1993, the prices of prescription
drug have been increasing at less than 4 percent annually,
only slightly above the general inflation rate and far below
the rate of increases in expenditures for prescription drugs

FIGURE 3

PHARMACEUTICAL EXPENDITURES AS A PERCENTAGE OF TOTAL
HEALTH EXPENDITURES BY COUNTRY, 1997

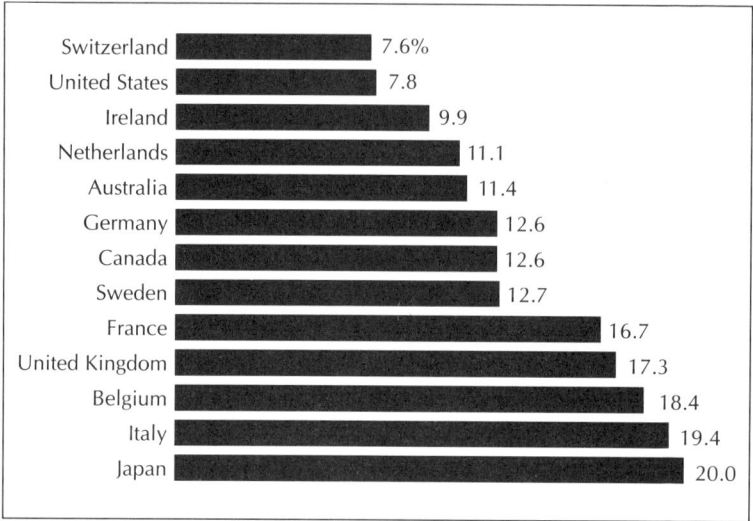

NOTE: 1996 pharmaceutical expenditures are reported for Australia
and Ireland.
SOURCE: OECD 1999.

(see figure 4).[9] According to surveys, higher prices for
existing drugs account for less than one-fourth of the
increased expenditures. The remaining increases result
from increased volume and particularly from a shift
toward more expensive drugs, which are usually newer on
the market.[10] Even the modest role for price increases is
exaggerated because measurements of pharmaceutical
price changes are upwardly biased: pharmaceutical price
indexes (like those for many other products) fail to adjust
for the higher quality of new drugs and the increased benefits from new uses for old drugs.[11]

The dominant role of new drugs in pharmaceutical
spending is reflected in the disproportionate increases in

FIGURE 4
INCREASES IN PRESCRIPTION DRUG PRICES AND THE GROWTH IN TOTAL EXPENDITURES, 1990–1998

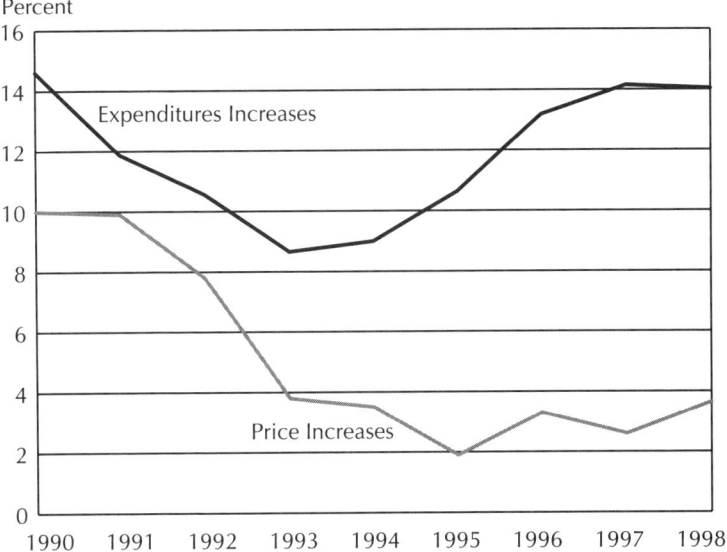

SOURCE: For increases in expenditures, HCFA 1999; for price increases, Bureau of Labor Statistics, CPI, All Urban Consumers, Prescription Drugs and Medical Supplies.

expenditures in the more innovative therapeutic areas. The largest increases between 1997 and 1998 involved heart medications and antidepressants, propelled by the success of the statin class of cholesterol-reducing drugs and of improved antidepressants. The path-breaking painkillers Celebrex and Vioxx boosted total sales for arthritis treatments in 1999, even as sales for older analgesics declined.[12]

Cost Savings from Pharmaceuticals
Reduced expenditures on other forms of health care have partially offset the increased expenditures on drugs

because drugs reduce many costly side effects and may prevent or simplify medical procedures. For example, H2 antagonists (Tagamet and other drugs that suppress stomach acid secretion) reduced the costs of surgery of gastrointestinal ulcers by more than half.[13] The use of "clot-busters" in treating strokes has reduced health care costs by about four times as much as the cost of the drug (not to mention the benefits to patients and families).[14] Schizophrenia drugs costing about $4,500 per year avoided about $73,000 a year in institutional treatment costs.[15] The medical literature abounds in studies documenting cost savings in health care from drug therapies for depression, congestive heart failure, asthma, strokes, migraine headaches, kidney disease, AIDS, and other illnesses and conditions.[16] An especially intriguing development is the recent, unexpected decline in Medicare hospitalizations, which has been accompanied by an even more surprising reduction in the severity of illness among hospital patients. Those developments have been paralleled by the growth in expenditures on heart drugs, which are disproportionately used by the elderly.[17]

Pharmaceuticals can also save money outside the health system. Much of the burden of illness falls on employers. For example, migraine headaches cost American employers an estimated $13 billion annually, compared with health care costs of only $1 billion.[18] Unsurprisingly, one study projected that better migraine treatments—another area with several new drugs on the market—will substantially reduce business costs.[19] Research has already demonstrated substantial savings in labor expenses and other business costs from drug therapies for depression, kidney disease, and other conditions.[20]

The Central Role of Consumer Benefits

The ability of pharmaceuticals to reduce the total expenditures for health care, as well as business costs, is important but secondary—and even something of a distraction. For it is patients and consumers who are gaining the most from modern drug therapy through better health, longer life, reduced pain and discomfort, and other blessings. The benefits to consumers from pharmaceutical advances figure in much of the discussion to follow, but it is useful to mention them here. New drugs are treating conditions that had been undertreated or even underdiagnosed. Such conditions include high blood pressure, elevated blood cholesterol, obesity, diabetes, depression and other mental illnesses, and osteoporosis. Many new treatments prevent sudden death and prolong life into old age. Almost certainly, the dramatic reduction in mortality from heart disease in the past thirty years, for example, is primarily due to improved medical treatments, including drug therapy.[21] The truly monumental benefits of these therapies have gone directly to consumers; whether the costs of health care have decreased or increased is unclear. At any rate, the benefits to consumers greatly exceed any increases in costs for health care.[22]

In addition, great progress in reducing pain and suffering has come from better pain relievers, drugs with fewer debilitating side effects, pills that replace injections, and treatments for migraines and osteoporosis. So-called lifestyle therapies—such as those for mild obesity, mild depression, allergies, hair loss, and impotence—are obviously of enormous value to consumers, notwithstanding that they add to their quality of life rather than health.

Foundations of Recent Advances in Research

Society is spending money to reap the early benefits from the "third revolution" in pharmaceutical research. The first was propelled by the serendipitous discovery of antibiotics and other natural substances in the 1940s. The second, in the 1960s and 1970s, was based on fundamental advances in our understanding of the mechanisms by which pharmaceuticals work in the body and led to such mainstays of today's drug treatments as ulcer treatments that block the secretion of stomach acid; beta-blockers, serum cholesterol-reducers, and other heart medications; and modern SSRI (selective serotonin reuptake inhibitors) antidepressants such as Prozac and its competitors.

Now the third pharmaceutical revolution—based partly on the explosive growth of molecular biology, including the decoding of the human genome itself—is underway. The new biology is married to the extraordinary analytical power of modern computers, plus a rich variety of computer-driven diagnostic instruments such as MRIs and CAT scans. The result is the unprecedented ease with which modern researchers can reveal the foundations of disease, explore promising molecules, and experiment with entirely new drug mechanisms. (The popular and academic literature in this area is voluminous and will not be reviewed here.)[23]

The third revolution, however, differs fundamentally from the first two. The earlier two were almost entirely based on science—as a result of dramatic discoveries about the basic biological mechanisms of infection and disease and their cure or alleviation through the injection or ingestion of pharmaceuticals. Today's revolution, though grounded on further, equally dramatic scientific advances, results also from innovations in institutions and markets that are coupling science and technology to the solution of practical problems in health care and disease management much more effectively than ever before.

One institutional innovation is a faster Food and Drug Administration. Since 1993, the percentage of new chemical entities approved in less than one year has increased from 20 percent to 50 percent, while the percentage approved after more than two years decreased from 45 percent to less than 5 percent, despite increases in the number of drugs submitted for approval.[24] After decades of lagging behind the Europeans, the FDA now appears to match the speed of the evolving drug approval system of the European Union.[25] However, demands for larger and more complex clinical trials have partly offset the greater regulatory speed.[26]

The FDA effort to reduce the "drug lag" has been greatly aided by an entirely new industry for conducting clinical trials, which emerged in the United States in the past decade. Large-scale drug testing was once run mainly by in-house researchers in collaboration with academic research centers, which supplied both physicians and patients. That tradition-bound system was more or less jettisoned in favor of a newer and much larger industry of primarily for-profit firms that recruit physicians and patients from nonacademic establishments and supervise the testing.[27] Although the new environment for clinical trials has aroused suspicions about the role of profits in drug testing, huge benefits have resulted. Efficiency has greatly increased. After being driven out by high costs, much of the drug testing has returned to the United States, where most new drugs are developed. More important, physicians who practice in the same environment in which most new drugs will be used now conduct the bulk of clinical testing and use subjects more representative of the general population than those in academic research centers. Presumably for that and other reasons, the American Medical Association has encouraged its members to participate in an activity that advances science while also supplementing physicians' earnings.[28]

The vast expansion in the enterprise of clinical testing provides more than just a faster way to get new drugs onto the market. It has also accelerated the rate at which new uses are found for existing drugs. New uses of drugs—including "off-label uses" that the FDA has not approved for inclusion in advertising or other promotional materials distributed by pharmaceutical firms—can be even more important than the original uses that led to FDA approval.[29] Off-label applications have long dominated cancer therapy and pediatrics; new uses are also crucial for more standardized treatments such as the statin-class cholesterol-reducing drugs, which have found their greatest applications through research conducted after the first statin drugs received approval for marketing.

Another essential element in the new environment of pharmaceutical research is the flexible corporate environment in the United States. Startup biotechnology firms can tap an aggressive financial community including venture capitalists while they utilize flexible labor markets and innovative arrangements for employee compensation. In addition, academia and government have developed methods for sharing intellectual property with both new and established pharmaceutical firms.

The final component of the new research environment is superior information. Managed care organizations and intermediaries such as pharmaceutical-benefit management firms create vast quantities of clinical data that, though usually not from randomized experimental designs used in per approval drug testing, may nonetheless possess great validity because the patients and situations involved are more typical of actual practice. Such data permit better and faster assessment of the safety of newly approved drugs because pharmaceutical firms and the FDA can take advantage of the prospect of superior postapproval surveillance for drug safety.[30] Hence the FDA has reported that recalls of new drugs have not increased despite the acceleration in new drug approvals.[31] The new data resources also permit rapid exploratory analysis for new uses and improved dosages of existing drugs. Thus research can take advantage not only of larger sample sizes but also of the greater external validity (that is, more realistic clinical environments) of nonrandomized trials.

That dramatic progress results from the confluence of pure science and broader developments in market and nonmarket institutions is hardly unique to pharmaceuticals. Consider the U.S. leadership regarding the Internet and its uses, including the burgeoning phenomenon of e-commerce. Where did that leadership come from? It is one thing to have at hand superior computer algorithms, lightning-fast microprocessors, and fiber-optic technology for telecommunications. But those technologies and the means for producing them spread quickly through developed economies around the world. What is available here, and no place else, is the combination of capital mobility and risk-taking, public willingness to invest in risky projects, flexible labor markets (in France, the government authorities raid software firms to make sure that managers are not working more than the statutory limit of thirty-five hours per week),[32] flexible compensation plans (stock options are still rare in Europe),[33] lightly regulated advertising and promotion (the advertising of discounts is illegal in Germany), rapid immigration of talented foreign engineers and entrepreneurs, and an absence of controls over prices or other essential elements of the core activities. The combination of technology with market institutions unleashed the Internet to explore applications undreamed of only a decade earlier. The parallel to modern pharmaceutical advances is striking.

We now turn to the results of the marriage of pharmaceutical science, institutions, and markets.

3

The Pharmaceutical Revolution Is Doing More Than Expected

The hallmark of the third pharmaceutical revolution is the ability to solve problems far more quickly than ever before. But each of the contributing elements—advances in biological science, in the technology of clinical trials, in the dissemination and collection of information, and so on—continues to evolve rapidly. We can expect even more striking advances in drug treatments over the next five to ten years.

Pharmaceutical research is an exercise in applied science; as such, its practical results depend strongly on the strength of collaborative activities in the marketplace. Current developments in health care and in other markets tend to amplify and hasten the impact of pharmaceutical breakthroughs. The effects of quicker and more efficient pharmaceutical research are therefore more extensive than one might think. New cures and palliatives for long-standing medical problems are only the first part of the story. Other parts include a far more competitive pricing environment, an astonishing expansion in the scope of drug therapy, and a corresponding escalation in the value of more vigorous dissemination of information to the medical community, patients, and consumers.

New Treatments for Old Problems

New medications for old problems are the most familiar results of recent pharmaceutical research. Medical journals and the popular press are full of accounts of new cures and palliatives. Examples include new treatments for adult-onset diabetes; manic-depression and other mental illnesses; hypertension, elevated cholesterol, and other heart problems; and migraine headaches, osteoporosis, and diabetes.[34]

Almost as important as new treatments are drugs that reduce side effects. Notable examples include the Cox-2 inhibitors and the SSRI class of antidepressants. The Cox-2 inhibitors are designed to suppress an enzyme that causes inflammation without suppressing a related enzyme (called Cox-1) that is needed to protect the stomach from developing ulcers. The advance is crucial because ulcers cause tens of thousands of deaths annually among those who take traditional pain relievers, which suppress both enzymes.[35] The first Cox-2 inhibitor, Celebrex, was introduced early in 1999 and became the best-selling new drug in history, while a competing brand, Vioxx, is doing nearly as well.[36] The SSRI antidepressants such as Prozac, Zolof, and Paxil appear no more effective than older tricyclic antidepressants at relieving depression. But the newer drugs employ a cleaner mechanism that interacts with a much narrower group of receptors in the brain. That process results in far fewer side effects and a much lower danger of overdose. The differences are so great that the medical profession considers the SSRI anti-depressants a nearly revolutionary advance in psychotropic drugs.[37] Other new drugs with important benefits in reduced side effects are newer heart medications and contraceptives.

Better patient compliance with drug regimens is also important. The monumental problem of inadequate compliance has transfixed the medical community for decades but has received scant attention from the general public. Research generally shows that a majority of individual therapeutic regimes are not fully complied with.[38] Causes range from cost and inconvenience to subtle or unpleasant side effects. Clearly, better compliance is a route to better therapy. An antidepressant that avoids weight gain, sweating, and dry mouth or a children's antibiotic taken once a day, instead of three or four times a day, can be as valuable as a new cure.[39] Appropriately, some of the most vigorous research and promotion focuses on mundane matters—such as ease of use—that can improve compliance. The consumer products firm Procter & Gamble, for example, is using its expertise in packaging to increase the effectiveness of a combination ulcer drug therapy.[40]

Finally, remarkable improvements in long-standing problems have occurred in the alleviation of pain and suffering. As noted, those include better analgesics, pills to replace injections, treatments for osteoporosis, and some of the so-called lifestyle therapies, such as mild obesity therapies.

Faster Competition

A less obvious benefit of the pharmaceutical research revolution is quicker and more intense competition, including more competition in prices. Just as in the computer and telecommunication markets, high-priced pharmaceutical innovations are under constant pressure from yet more innovation. The period of one-brand dominance for an innovating drug within a breakthrough therapeutic category has unmistakably shortened.[41] Inderal, the first beta blocker for heart disease, was introduced in 1965; its first competitor, Lopressor, came thirteen years later, in 1978. Tagamet, the first H2 antagonist (stomach acid suppressor) for ulcers, was introduced in 1977, followed by Zantac six years later. In the 1980s, breakthrough drugs included the ACE inhibitor Capoten for heart disease, the allergy-fighting antihistamine Seldane, the AIDS drug AZT, the first "statin" drug for high cholesterol (Mevacor), and the first SSRI for depression, Prozac. In each case, a competitor appeared within four years (five, in the case of Capoten).

Research moved even faster in the 1990s. Diflucan, a new antifungal, was approved in 1990 and met competition from Sporax in 1992. Recombinate, a new blood treatment for hemophiliacs, arrived in 1992 and faced competition the next year. The first protease inhibitor for HIV (Invirase) encountered a competitive market within a few months. The Cox-2 inhibitor Celebrex for arthritis pain enjoyed only a few months as the lone brand before it faced Vioxx in a battle over the arthritis pain market that quickly brought price cuts.[42] Highly visible battles are raging among the statin class of cholesterol-reducing drugs as well as among the modern generation of antidepressants, including Prozac, Paxil, Zoloft, and Celexa.[43] Before 1997, no useful treatments existed for adult-onset diabetes, a devastating and extremely costly disease. Now three are competing in terms of their safety profiles as well as efficacy.[44] Such acceleration in competition has not escaped the business press, which notes a proliferation of new brands in the pipeline for more breakthrough categories of drugs.[45] For example, a new clot buster is being prepared to compete with tPA, the biotech drug that was the first treatment ever devised for strokes. The new drug would double the time window for reversing the effects of strokes from the current three hours to about six.[46]

The notion of faster competition brings up an important related point about the prices of new and of older drugs. Some widely cited studies simply compare the prices of new drugs with those of the drugs that they replace, almost as if the new drugs did not provide a substantial therapeutic or other improvement.[47] But from the standpoint of medical care and other relevant criteria such as ease of use, the new drugs are typically of higher quality—sometimes much higher. In the highly competitive markets for beta blockers, ACE inhibitors, and statin cholesterol-reducing drugs—all used to treat or prevent heart disease—the market pioneers have found their market share eroding, partly because of aggressive pricing from new entrants and partly because manufacturers of new drugs typically seek a market share by providing reduced side effects or greater ease of use.[48] Hence, research strongly suggests that perceived increases in pharmaceutical prices would almost certainly be greatly moderated, if not erased altogether, after adjusting for quality.[49]

Expanded Scope of Pharmaceutical Therapy

If pharmaceutical research became more efficient but nothing else changed, we might expect essentially the same drugs to come to the market but to do so faster and at lower cost.[50] But the ability to create new products faster and more cheaply opens new opportunities. The situation is analogous to the development of the microprocessor, which facilitated the production of existing computer designs but also permitted new designs for entirely new applications. Because the benefits of computer processing expanded even faster than costs declined, total computer expenditures rapidly escalated. Software experienced the same pattern; revenues escalated even as the costs of writing programs dropped. Worldwide software sales through independent sellers have increased even more rapidly than pharmaceutical sales: from $9 billion in 1987 to $28 billion in 1995.[51] Similar patterns apply to closely related products such as disk storage and printers and in other technologically innovative areas such as telecommunications and transportation: per unit costs dropped, applications expanded, and total expenditures increased.

The revolution in pharmaceutical research technology is also spawning entirely new areas of application, as is evident from the rapid advances in treating illnesses and conditions that had once proved more or less intractable. Examples include drugs that reverse obesity and thus provide a means for preventing or treating Type II diabetes; better treatments for depression, bipolar disorders, and other mental illnesses; and cholesterol-reducing drugs that offer an alternative to angioplasty for coronary heart disease.[52] Many conditions newly amenable to drug therapy are not necessarily disabling, but are rather like impediments or handicaps that were endured, often at great cost, because they could not be treated. Many such conditions are extremely common. Thus, the accelerating revolution in pharmaceutical research has brought many people into the health care system for the treatment of conditions that otherwise might have remained untreated or even undiagnosed for years.

A second, overlapping trend is the accelerated development of drugs that prevent illness by treating risk factors. Examples include the statin class of cholesterol-reducing drugs, treatments for hypertension and mild or moderate obesity, and the prevention of osteoporosis. In each case, pharmaceutical and epidemiological research has simultaneously expanded the proportion of the population at risk and demonstrated the ability of drug therapy to reduce that risk. According to recent estimates, obesity affects approximately 55 percent of the adult U.S. population; the combination of obesity, diabetes, hypertension, and elevated cholesterol places some 75 percent of those adults at risk.[53] Such research is altering the boundaries between lifestyle and treatable medical conditions. The Agency for Health Care Policy and Research recently noted that "better epidemiological data has allowed us to move from calling something 'just normal variation' to 'risk factor' to 'disease.'"[54]

A third trend, overlapping the first two, is the development of pharmaceuticals that do not necessarily reduce medical risk at all but do permit lifestyle improvements. Those include treatments for pain, mild obesity, mild depression, allergies, impotence, and hair loss and are often of great value to consumers (and perhaps to employers, who may see increased productivity). Moreover, that value may affect a tremendous number of people who would otherwise not seek drug treatment or perhaps any form of medical treatment.

Increased Value of Advertising and Promotion

The public, the medical community, health care organizations, and others have blamed pharmaceutical advertising and promotion for raising costs and inducing unnecessary or unwise usage.[55] Most of these accusations arose not from systematic analysis but from the simple fact that direct-to-consumer advertising of prescription drugs has become far more prominent since 1997, when the FDA relaxed its rules for television advertising of drugs directly to consumers.[56]

A more complete assessment of pharmaceutical advertising should take into account the fact that advertising is a way to disseminate information while pursuing competitive goals. Hence its importance and effects depend strongly on the information needs of the marketplace. The new prominence of pharmaceutical advertising will be seen as yet another byproduct of the advances in pharmaceutical research.

The New Environment of Pharmaceutical Information. The rapid expansion of drug therapy has widened the gap between what research has found and what physicians, patients, and consumers know. The medical community has responded with journal articles and newsletters, medical education seminars, and formal statements on drug therapy. The past few years have seen a steady series of practice guidelines and consensus statements from physician organizations and public health groups on treating obesity, elevated cholesterol, depression, osteoporosis, and other conditions. Those documents are designed to provide physicians and health care providers with guidance on the practical implications of therapeutic advances. But even public health organizations find it difficult to keep up with the science. For example, a Dutch working group on heart disease treatment, after issuing a guidance on cholesterol treatment in 1998, found it necessary to issue a 1999 revision based on new pharmaceutical research.[57]

Physician and consumer information about new therapies typically lags well behind the practice guides that have been issued—the American Medical Association recently emphasized that point in a newsletter article, "Not-in-Practice Guidelines."[58] The same point is often emphasized in the consensus statements themselves, which deplore the extent to which physicians are failing to keep up with changes dictated by new drug regimes. Obesity, diabetes, asthma, depression, manic-depressive disorders, osteoporosis, elevated serum cholesterol, hypertension, and heart disease have all been described in the medical literature as being widely untreated, under-treated, or undiagnosed.[59] A *JAMA* article by the consensus panel on depression, for example, concluded that "there is still an enormous gap between our knowledge about the correct diagnosis and treatment of depression and the actual treatment that is being received in this country." Recent research on osteoporosis suggests that 20 percent of sixty-five-year-olds and half of eighty-year-olds are at risk for broken bones and may benefit from medical treatment.[60]

The Role of Advertising. Advertising has always been a basic market response to information deficits because it harnesses private incentives to cover the costs of disseminating knowledge. Perhaps the most vivid demonstration came from the torrent of health claims for foods launched in the mid-1980s. Food advertising about health and nutrition improved consumer information and induced manufacturers to improve their products.[61] Clearly, the incentives to disseminate information are strongest when brands incorporate unique information that does not apply to competing brands, but the health claims illustrate the value of advertising in spreading knowledge even when the crucial information is not specific to a single brand.

The health care and medical technology markets are no exception. The documented gaps between research findings and physician practices are notoriously difficult to close.[62] Pharmaceutical advertising and promotion are therefore essential tools for narrowing these gaps. Manufacturers have incentives to focus on such gaps because of the prospect that better information will encourage physicians to prescribe their brands. The content of advertising to physicians reflects such thinking. For example, the first advertisement in the November 25, 1999, *New England Journal of Medicine* was for an ACE inhibitor, a class of drugs that has been documented as greatly underprescribed to prevent heart attacks.[63] The first ad in that week's *JAMA* was for an antidepressant, another underprescribed drug category.[64] Advertisements for the statin class of cholesterol-reducing drugs are a staple of medical journals, even as a *New York Times* story about a March 1999 meeting of the American College of Cardiology carried the headline "Cholesterol-Cutting Drugs Go Unused."[65] When the Cox-2 inhibitors for arthritis pain were first marketed, they were supported by large forces of detailers (pharmaceutical sales representatives who visit physicians and health care providers.)[66] Antihypertension drugs, also underprescribed, are also heavily advertised.[67]

Sensibly, much pharmaceutical promotion focuses on closing the most consequential gaps in information between the research community and practitioners. The high cost of pharmaceutical promotion—about $6 billion during 1998, including media advertising, detailing, and other activities—reflects the cost of summarizing and delivering essential information where it can do the most good and repeating the information sufficiently for assimilation and use.

Pharmaceutical promotion, like promotion generally, has the important byproduct of providing information about competing brands (other cholesterol-reducing drugs, for example), competing products (foods instead of drugs, for example), and even competing activities such as exercise and dietary improvement. That byproduct is an inevitable consequence of the environment in which pharmaceutical advertising takes place. For example, when firms promote drugs to prevent osteoporosis, diabetes, or heart disease (by reducing hypertension or serum cholesterol), they necessarily emphasize prevention itself. But consensus statements and practice guidelines on the prevention of heart disease, diabetes, and many other conditions typically specify diet, exercise, and other measures as the first line of therapy before the drugs that are so heavily advertised. A recent British Hypertension Society guide began with the injunction to "use non-pharmacological measures in all hypertensive and borderline hypertensive people"—meaning exercise and dietary changes—before it discussed drug therapy.[68] Similarly, a *Drug Benefit Trends* update on osteoporosis prevention and treatment began by discussing diet and exercise before turning to drug therapy.[69]

Even when drug therapy is called for, physicians need not stick with the brands being advertised. They have heard about competing brands, too, and they are generally familiar with older drugs, including "generics" that compete with off-patent branded drugs. Physicians tend to prescribe from a small and slowly changing battery of pharmaceuticals—a well-documented tendency that even vigorous branded promotion can overcome only with difficulty.[70] And physicians often respond to pharmaceutical promotion by choosing an older substitute instead of the promoted brand or even—when diet or exercise is the preferred solution—by avoiding pharmaceuticals altogether.[71]

Consumers also need information about new drugs. Many new therapies will languish unless consumers seek out physicians to ask about new treatments, improvements, and the like. Advertising directly to consumers, like promotion to physicians, can yield great benefits.[72]

Consumer advertising of prescription drugs has mounted rapidly since the FDA relaxed its rules in 1997 to permit television advertising. Total media expenditures between March 1998 and March 1999 were estimated at some $1.5 billion[73] and were nearly $1 billion for the first six months of 1999.[74] Most advertising was devoted to drugs treating conditions for which consumers are unlikely to seek medical attention on their own: allergy medications that avoid drowsiness, the statin cholesterol-reducing drugs, and antidepressants.[75]

Sometimes a new drug requires changes far beyond hospitals or physicians' offices. Clinical trials showed that tPA, a biotechnology clot buster that had been approved for breaking up the clots causing heart attacks, could also cure the most common form of stroke (which is caused by a clot in an artery leading to the brain)—provided that the drug was administered within three hours after the stroke. No treatment for stroke had existed. The American Medical Association therefore immediately issued a statement: "New Drug for Stroke Only as Good as Systems That Go Along with It: Changes in healthcare systems and education of general public are key."[76] The medical system had concentrated on providing comfort rather than immediate hospitalization for stroke victims; in fact, most hospitals did not even have protocols for acute stroke treatment. In the new environment created by tPA, consumers must recognize the symptoms of a stroke and then must obtain immediate assistance. Family physicians, paramedics, and emergency room personnel must understand the necessity of getting a victim to a hospital in time to conduct necessary diagnostics and then administer tPA within the short window of opportunity for dissolving the clot before the brain is permanently damaged.[77] The manufacturer of tPA therefore undertook the task of communicating the basic facts about stroke symptoms and the necessity for quick action—using advertising in medical journals aimed at physicians plus direct-to-consumer advertising, including full-page newspaper ads with the heading "425,000 Strokes Are Uncalled for."[78]

The United States is the only large developed nation to permit direct-to-consumer advertising of prescription drugs. Resistance to direct-to-consumer advertising may be weakening in the European Union, however. A recent *Lancet* editorial stated, "The time is right for an extension of direct-to-public advertising for prescription-only medicines from the USA to other countries, at least on a trial basis."[79]

Consumer advertising of prescription drugs, like promotion directed at physicians, tends to provide essential information that would otherwise move far more slowly from the research community to patients and consumers. Again, many of the most-promoted drugs are for conditions for which the first line of therapy is not pharmaceuticals at all or for which generics or alternative brands may be acceptable. The ability of advertising to improve markets by providing valuable information is one reason why the Federal Trade Commission and the European Union (along with the U.S. Supreme Court) strongly support nondeceptive advertising as a protected form of speech.[80]

Finally, direct-to-consumer advertising can yield benefits that are more or less unique to pharmaceuticals. Advertising can encourage consumers to ask their physicians about problems that do not appear to be medical symptoms but may be serious and treatable conditions. An obvious example is impotence, which may be caused by heart disease or other illnesses; a Viagra ad may cause someone to receive needed treatment but may not sell any Viagra at all.[81]

How Advertising Encourages Clinical Research. The ability to promote a health benefit can provide an incentive to undertake research to document such a benefit. The statin class of cholesterol-reducing drugs provides an example. In 1989, a drug manufacturer wanting to compete more successfully with the market leader began clinical trials at a cost of nearly $50 million to demonstrate that its drug would prevent heart attacks in people who had not been regarded as at risk because they had only moderately elevated cholesterol levels and were otherwise healthy. After six years, the research demonstrated a 31 percent reduction in heart attacks, which led to FDA approval to market the drug for preventing heart attacks.[82] As a result, sales increased for that particular drug brand. Also, attention was bound to increase on the prevention of heart attacks through diet and other means of reducing serum cholesterol.

Most significant, this and other statin drug trials provided the first conclusive proof that reducing blood cholesterol could prevent heart attacks and save lives. An August 1999 *Annals of Internal Medicine* reviewed the statin drug trials and noted that "the long-term clinical efficacy for the primary and secondary prevention of cardiovascular outcomes has been difficult to establish because of the enormous sample sizes and lengthy durations such trials require." The article described how the statin trials, considered in combination, had at last demonstrated the validity of the long-hypothesized connection between cholesterol reduction and heart disease mortality.[83] The significance of these findings is illustrated by the fact that between 1989 and 1993, a well-known academic researcher wrote a series of popular books and articles attacking the medical profession for wasting resources by acting on the "mistaken" hypothesis that heart disease could be prevented by reducing serum cholesterol, particularly through drug therapy.[84]

The advent of direct-to-consumer advertising of prescription drugs has further strengthened the incentives for manufacturers to conduct research on drugs already on the market. Research on existing drugs accounts for about one-quarter of pharmaceutical clinical trials. The goal is to learn more about exactly which consumers can benefit the most from the various characteristics of ongoing drug therapy. Indeed, a pharmaceutical advertising agency had essentially that purpose in mind when it recently acquired a firm specializing in clinical trials.[85]

4

The Budgeting Problem with Pharmaceuticals

What is the perspective of the purchasers of pharmaceuticals—primarily governments, managed care organizations, and health insurers? It is only natural for such organizations to think in terms of future budgets for spending on pharmaceuticals. As explained later, such budgeting plays a central role in the Clinton administration's proposed Medicare drug benefit. Unfortunately, the notion of dictating future drug therapy budgets raises serious difficulties.

The gains in pharmaceutical research technology make it almost impossible to predict the desired levels of spending on pharmaceuticals for more than a year or two. We cannot know what new drug therapies will become available, how well they will work, or what populations might benefit from new or existing therapies. The difficulty is apparent from the highly uneven nature of recent increases in drug expenditures. Some therapeutic categories increased by 20 percent or more within a single year while others remained stable or even declined.[86] But the unevenness results not from shifting expenditures from one category to another, but from taking advantage of new opportunities as they appear: spending has escalated where new benefits from drug therapy have emerged. In some cases, spending increased not because of the introduction of new types of pharmaceuticals but because of the discovery that existing drugs provided benefits that were largely unexpected until the results of large postapproval clinical trials began to emerge. A notable example is the use of statin-class cholesterol-reducing drugs to treat a mild elevation of serum cholesterol.[87]

As yet other therapeutic areas see the arrival of innovative drugs, the benefits of those new treatments will trigger further surges in pharmaceutical spending with no expectation of offsetting declines elsewhere in drug costs. Indeed, that situation will occur if and when cancer cures, dementia treatments, and other long-awaited developments emerge. After all, molecular biology and allied disciplines are supplying an endless series of tantalizing leads. Cancer therapies might be tailored to a patient's genes and yield treatments far superior to anything yet achieved.[88] Researchers are honing in on leptin, a molecule essential to controlling appetite (and therefore preventing obesity).[89] Scientists at several pharmaceutical firms are exploring the discovery of an enzyme that apparently plays a crucial role in Alzheimer's disease in the hopes of devising a preventative or cure despite the daunting complexity of brain science.[90] Improvements in imaging devices and other instruments are opening the way to a better understanding of the neurological foundations of depression and other mental illnesses.[91]

When or where such breakthroughs will occur or how valuable they will be is impossible to predict. Long-term budgeting for pharmaceutical expenditures is therefore impossible in the sense of specifying a reasonable amount to spend on pharmaceuticals five or ten years ahead.

An equally important impediment to pharmaceutical budgeting is the recent expansion of drug therapy beyond the traditional functions of acute health care organizations. Again, no one can know how much should be spent five or ten years from now on the primary prevention of chronic illnesses, where the cholesterol-reducing drugs have achieved such gratifying success. The same is true of spending to alleviate conditions that defy categorization into lifestyle improvements or health improvements. Those areas encompass treatments for moderate pain, mild obesity, mild depression, and other conditions that health care facilities do not normally treat.

If health care budgeting imposes strict limits on spending, rather than using a more flexible approach such as providing partial support for spending, it would prevent consumers from obtaining treatments that would be worth more than their cost. The basic criteria for the value of new drugs should be the benefits to consumers rather than the benefits to governments or other providers of health care. Recent developments in pharmaceuticals reflect that view, for the value of pharmaceuticals to consumers is increasing even faster than the value to health care organizations.

It is essential to maintain consumer willingness to pay for new treatments as the basic market signal for further investments in pharmaceutical research. Only market prices can accomplish that. The next issue is price controls.

5
The Threat of Price Controls

Criticism of pharmaceutical prices naturally provokes discussions of price controls. The United States is perhaps the only large nation that does not impose government controls over drug prices in one way or another, although price controls are already in place in many other parts of the health care system. Press accounts routinely mention the possibility of controls over pharmaceutical prices.[92] This section addresses four topics: the reasons pharmaceutical price controls are politically popular and are often used; the new elements of risk in pharmaceutical research; the diverse effects of price controls; and the ease with which controls could emerge from an expansion of the current Medicare system to cover pharmaceuticals. Chapter 6 addresses what, if anything, Congress should do about pharmaceutical prices.

Why Pharmaceutical Price Controls Are Politically Attractive

Three factors make pharmaceuticals a perennial target for price controls. One is the peculiar cost structure of pharmaceutical development: high upfront research expenditures and low marginal costs of manufacturing and distribution. That structure ensures that new drugs will be sold at a price that far exceeds the costs of production, that is, at what appears to be a fat profit margin. The second factor is the lengthy time-lag between incurring costs and recouping them through sales. In turn, the lag guarantees that anyone in a position to control prices can easily ignore the true costs. The third factor is the unique nature of the product of pharmaceutical research. The real output from research is a piece of information: one particular chemical entity cures a disease, while thousands of similar chemicals are useless or worse. That information is the only reason for the value of the drug. Once the information has been revealed, however, anyone can use it. Generic drugs (that is, off-patent drugs) from nonresearch firms can then compete successfully with brands from manufacturers whose research had demonstrated the efficacy of those drugs.

Such circumstances provide the government with an opportunity to give voters the appearance of receiving something for nothing. Capping drug prices would neither halt the supply of existing drugs nor destroy the supply of knowledge about their use. The real costs of controls would remain generally unseen or would at least be delayed until the deleterious impact of controls emerged.

The pharmaceutical industry's unusual pattern of profits is also important, in part because of how profits are calculated. Standard accounting rules yield inflated measures of pharmaceutical returns on investment because they fail to calculate investment in a way that includes a full measure of research and development costs. The pharmaceutical research enterprise consequently appears more profitable than it actually is.[93] Another factor is the disproportionately large profits from a few so-called blockbuster brands. Those obscure the losses from the far more numerous financial failures. A detailed examination of pharmaceutical research, development, and marketing has shown that almost all promising chemical entities fail at some point during clinical testing. Moreover, most of the drugs that do make it to market fail to cover their average research and development costs. A few blockbuster drugs make up the difference.[94] Those few lucrative brands attract attention and suggest the existence of unseemly profits. But those profits from a few select brands appear essential to support the entire array of new drugs.

Another factor that encourages price controls is the dominant role of third-party payments. In the United States, third-party reimbursement is encouraged because health insurance premiums paid by employers are exempt from taxation. That exemption is an accident of history and a fallout from price controls. Employers that wished to raise wages under the price controls of World War II resorted to adding fringe benefits, including health insurance, as a way to get around wage ceilings.[95] Those benefits were not taxed; the situation has persisted since. Thus, health care is cheaper when it is funneled through employer-paid insurance than when it is paid for directly. Insurance firms, rather than consumers directly, have paid essentially the entire increase in nongovernmental pharmaceutical expenditures since 1990. Thus the proportion of prescription drugs paid through insurance and other third-party mechanisms increased from 37 percent in 1990 to 75 percent in 1998.[96] That circumstance, combined with increased spending on new drugs, has prompted widespread public attention to the role of pharmaceuticals in rising premiums for health insurance and managed care.[97]

The impact of the peculiar cost structure of pharmaceuticals, combined with the motivation of third-party payers, is evident in other industrialized economies, where government or government-mandated organizations dominate health care. Those organizations have felt financial pressure from the advent of new and more valuable drugs. An astonishing variety of price controls has resulted.[98] Some nations, especially smaller or poorer ones, have negotiated extremely low prices for drugs that were expensive to develop. Even wealthy nations, such as Canada and many European Union members, have demonstrated that they can often negotiate prices that are well below the long-run development costs but still high enough to yield a short-run profit for manufacturers.[99]

Those arrangements may be less permanent than they appear, however. They can persist only if the nations with low prices can prevent the exportation of drugs to nations with uncontrolled prices or higher controlled prices. Maintaining a ban on pharmaceutical exports has been difficult in the European Union because of its lack of border controls. The advent of Internet purchasing and other means for transborder shipments may soon end multitiered pricing. When that happens, nations that enjoy prices far below those set by a free market will be unable to maintain their advantage. The same outcome could eventually happen to the impoverished nations of Asia and Africa, where consumers would no longer be able to purchase pharmaceuticals that the developed world takes for granted. In the meantime, however, low marginal costs invite price controls in many nations.

The New Risk Environment for
Pharmaceutical Research

The new research environment has added important new elements to the risk environment of pharmaceutical research as a byproduct of the dramatic exploration of entirely new areas of application.[100] Manufacturers that venture into new territory are less certain of what they will find and less confident of what it will be worth when they find it—they face new uncertainties over both supply and demand.

Demand. Of the numerous factors that create uncertainty over the demand for new drugs, two stand out. First, many new drugs address conditions that had not been systematically treated. Data on the prevalence, health consequences, and social costs are sparse because conditions that are not treated tend not to be studied. Second, even if one does know the number of those suffering from a condition and the health consequences of that condition, we still may have only a vague idea of what people are willing to pay for the drugs that alleviate those conditions. Uncertainty over the health benefits from a new drug is therefore one problem, and uncertainty over what consumers are willing to pay for those benefits is another.

Obesity is a good example of the uncertainty surrounding the health benefits of potential treatments. The prevalence of obesity varies with demographic changes, cultural differences, diet, and lifestyle. Estimates of the health risks associated with obesity have changed dramatically in the wake of new research, with new definitions of clinical obesity.[101] A recurring question in recent research on obesity is whether to treat the condition itself rather than its medical consequences.[102] When treating obesity directly, non-drug treatments are normally the first option. But the persistence of obesity—despite widespread popular and medical advice to exercise and eat better—indicates that drug treatment has potential importance.[103] Even with drugs, success requires considerable personal motivation. Obesity strikingly parallels smoking: the effort to reduce mortality from heart disease by persuading smokers to quit has been generally ineffective and has left physicians looking to pharmaceutical treatment for progress.[104] The split in the medical community over pursuing any drug therapy at all for obesity strongly suggests that the magnitude of the potential benefits from obesity drugs is highly uncertain. No one knows what proportion of the population would respond to treatments yet to be developed or to new initiatives for behavioral changes or how many would spontaneously alter their diet and other behaviors without any treatment.

Quite different from the question of health benefits from new drugs is the matter of what health care organizations, employers, and consumers are willing to pay for those benefits. Obesity, chronic pain, depression, and other conditions newly amenable to treatment involve subjective discontent. The same holds true for such potential advances as the development of oral replacements for injections of insulin and other large-molecule drugs (a "godsend" for diabetics, according to the president of the American Diabetic Association, Gerald Bernstein), the ability to save ovaries during cancer treatment, and other improvements in the administration of drugs.[105] Even so, measuring consumer valuations of reductions in pain and suffering is a notoriously difficult task.[106] The demand for many new drug treatments ultimately depends on such subjective consumer preferences and on the transmission of those preferences throughout the health care system.

Consider the enduring mystery of the market demand for drug therapies that encourage compliance with the therapeutic regimes prescribed by physicians. We know that noncompliance defeats many medications. We also know that better drugs, improved delivery systems, and even counseling can reduce noncompliance.[107] But it is hard to predict the health benefits of drugs and delivery systems that increase the probability of compliance (itself an unexplored topic); it is even more difficult to predict what health care providers and patients would be willing to pay for those benefits.

Supply. The costs of developing new treatments are also shrouded in uncertainty. New research tools notwithstanding, failure is still the norm when researchers attack problems that have remained unsolved for decades. Research on diabetes is a good example. One promising line of attack—a drug to prevent nerve damage from diabetes rather than attacking the illness itself—met unexpected failure in clinical trials in the late 1980s, yet seemed on the verge of success early in 1999. Clinical trials failed again in August 1999; the news media reported that a manufacturer was forced to halt trials on an expected blockbuster new brand.[108] Despite progress in other lines of attack, the revolution in the treatment of diabetes lies ahead.[109]

Another example is gene therapy, a technique designed to alter cancer cells at a genetic level. It is hard to conjure a more fruitful application of modern genetics than physically correcting the genetic abnormalities that cause disease. Gene therapy has attracted some well-qualified pioneers. After a few researchers at the National Institutes of Health obtained promising preliminary results, several pharmaceutical firms attacked the crucial problem of delivering the necessary carriers to exactly the right cells. They have yet to succeed. After nearly a billion dollars on laboratory experiments and small-scale clinical trials, no marketable drugs are in sight.[110] Nonetheless, research continues despite highly publicized setbacks.[111]

We know from other markets the formidable difficulties in predicting the consequences of rapidly changing conditions. No one can anticipate with any precision how much crude oil will be found, or where, in the wake of declining exploration costs or increased petroleum prices.[112] As research technology on pharmaceuticals advances, firms possess only a vague knowledge of what they or their competitors will find when they venture into vast new areas of research. These explorations promise yet more uncertainty. The gains in research technology represent a confluence of several independent factors that are highly uncertain and change rapidly: biological science, instrumentation, the creation and analysis of health care data, and the growing role of managed care and intermediaries such as pharmaceutical benefit management firms. All those factors involve trends that are difficult to predict. After examining such emerging developments as biochips (which are similar to computer chips but are composed of tiny strands of DNA, with the goal of assessing such things as which drugs are likely to attack a cancer cell), one is struck by the fact that the practical applications of molecular biology are in their infancy.[113] Estimates of the scientific or financial returns from additional research are therefore highly uncertain.

What Price Controls Do

The potential harm from price controls is far more varied and extensive than most people realize. Most harm is either difficult to predict or hidden from view when it occurs; moreover, dismantling controls can be extremely difficult. The most obvious problem is the disincentives for research and development. Other difficulties, equally dangerous if less obvious, include an inevitable drift toward ever more complicated controls, the entrenchment of vested interests, and the inability of any controls system to handle the complex market activities that are essential to progress in the modern pharmaceutical research enterprise.

Price Controls and Research Incentives. Advocates of price controls in the United States presumably wish to establish reasonable pharmaceutical prices or profits without impeding the development of useful new pharmaceuticals. That approach is extremely dangerous. What is a reasonable reward for solving research problems that have remained unsolved for decades? What is a cure for breast cancer worth, and what will it cost? The only reliable way to find out is to develop a drug that works (albeit presumably with serious side effects and other flaws) and then learn its worth to patients and their health insurance firms. Surely pharmaceutical firms would be reluctant to gamble a billion dollars or more in a highly uncertain search for a breast cancer cure if they believed that the Department of Health and Human Services might rule that the new drug's price was unreasonably high.

One danger from price controls is therefore almost universally recognized: the likelihood that price controls would drastically reduce research. The market's reaction to the Clinton administration's 1993 health care proposal amply demonstrates the reality of that danger. The plan would have allowed the Department of Health and Human Services to set prices of new breakthrough drugs.[114] The impact on research efforts was predictable. From 1981 through 1993, annual increases in the U.S. pharmaceutical industry R&D budget averaged 11 percent (in deflated dollars) and never dropped below 7 percent until 1994, when the industry faced President Clinton's health care plan. Then the increase in R&D expenditures dropped to 3 percent in 1994 and 4 percent in 1995. In 1996, after Congress had decisively defeated the administration's health care plan, the spending increases for research and development resumed and have averaged about 11 percent since 1995 (see figure 5). As other advanced nations have implemented pharmaceutical price controls, the locus of research has moved steadily to the United States, where firms produced all ten of the worldwide best-selling drugs.[115]

There is no substitute for the profit motive for inducing and guiding research. The worst action would be to erect a ceiling on the rewards for solving the toughest problems in medical science: preventing Alzheimer's; curing schizophrenia; reversing heart disease; striking without error at cancer cells; reducing the estimated 350,000 deaths annually from obesity; preventing 10,000 amputations a year from poor circulation, nerve damage, and other consequences of diabetes;[116] delineating the physiological foundations of neurological diseases like multiple sclerosis and Parkinson's; discovering new antibiotics for tuberculosis; finding AIDS cures that work in the long run; creating the next generation of antidepressants for the 60 percent of patients who cannot or do not use existing antidepressants;[117] developing vaccines for AIDS, malaria, and other infections; and solving quality-of-life problems with can-

FIGURE 5

Annual Percentage Changes in Pharmaceutical Research and Development, United States, 1980–1999

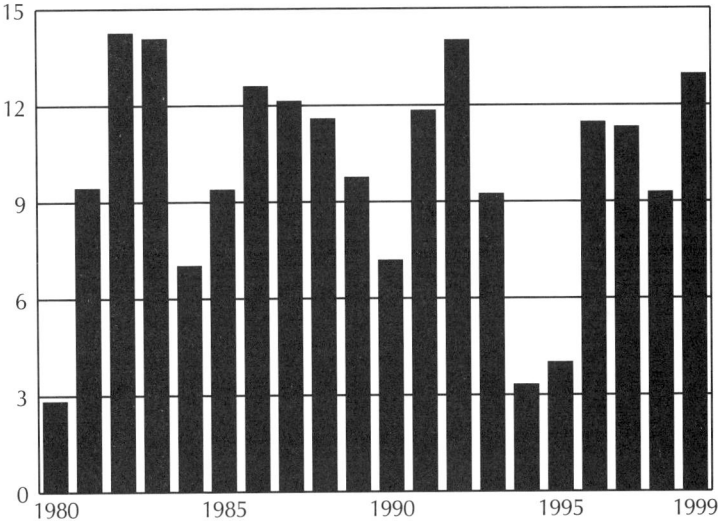

NOTE: All amounts were deflated before calcuations.
SOURCE: PhRMA 1999.

cer therapies that do not destroy ovaries, or insulin and biotech pills to replace injections.

The effects of controls on research incentives are apparent from worldwide trends. Because India and other underdeveloped nations have permitted domestic manufacturers to ignore international patents, pharmaceutical firms cannot protect their property rights to new drugs in those nations. The situation has encouraged low prices for modern antidepressants, heart medications, and other drugs developed for advanced economies but has completely forestalled the development of drugs specifically needed in India and other nations with unique sets of illnesses.

Malaria is an apposite example. That devastating illness, killing tens of millions annually, has been a forgotten stepchild in worldwide pharmaceutical research. A recent United Nations initiative in partnership with the pharmaceutical industry is motivated by the desire "to keep research in antimalarial drugs from ending because of the drugs' poor commercial potential."[118]

Why would a drug to be used by hundreds of millions or even billions of people have poor commercial potential? The irony and the obvious impact of pricing freedom on research incentives are tragically obvious. In the United States, an orphan-drug law permits manufacturers to obtain special patent protection for older drugs if they can find a cure for diseases that are so rare that firms would not ordinarily pursue cures through the FDA's onerous drug approval system. The law has been acclaimed for bringing more than 100 drugs to market to help victims who number a few thousand or less.[119]

Yet the millions who suffer from malaria wait for similar advances.[120] Any pharmaceutical firm that developed a malaria vaccine could expect that the major affected nations, most with a poor record for respecting property rights to pharmaceuticals, would quickly declare that public health is more important than pharmaceutical profits. Then they would establish compulsory licensing or some other means to force the drug to be sold at a price that ignores the costs and risks of the investments that produced the drug. By putting public health ahead of pharmaceutical industry profits, the third world nations have achieved neither. A medical advocacy group recently noted that of 1,223 new compounds developed during 1975–1997, only 11 were for tropical diseases.[121]

Research disincentives are far from the only problem with price controls, however. If incentives were the sole difficulty, a complex but far-sighted arrangement might carefully set prices that would avoid the unseemly prices and profits that aroused interest in controls in the first place, without impeding socially desirable research. But other inevitable problems in price controls reveal the futility of such an effort.

Complexity and the Entrenchment of Vested Interests. The history of price controls demonstrates that once in place, controls have a life of their own.[122] The unavoidable tendency toward mind-numbing complexity became obvious during the wage and price controls of the Nixon administration, even for such apparently highly standardized products as refined gasoline. The Medicare system itself is another prime example with arbitrary, contentious, and highly detailed controls over payments for medical technology, physicians, and other services. Nations that have already implemented pharmaceutical price controls provide numerous striking examples of amazingly complex and arbitrary controls.[123]

Perhaps even more important is the tendency for powerful parties to work the controls system to their advantage and, if possible, to the disadvantage of competitors. Price controls on pharmaceuticals in Japan and, to a lesser extent, in France are designed to protect domestic pharmaceutical manufacturers. In both cases, these arrangements work to the disadvantage of consumers, particularly in Japan, where many of the most effective drug therapies for cancer, heart disease, and other conditions are simply unavailable. Not only do manufacturers gain from controls but so do other parties, notably physicians in Japan and bureaucracies everywhere who carry out the crucial job of setting prices and otherwise administering controls.[124]

Unsurprisingly, price controls tend to persist even when they cause obvious problems. Many of the Nixon administration controls, notably in the petroleum industry, lasted for years after the overall program was officially dismantled. Emergency rent controls enacted in New York in World War II are still in effect for hundreds of thousands of housing units.[125] Price controls on automobile insurance have persisted in Massachusetts even though they yield some of the highest rates in the nation.[126] Airline price controls under the Civil Aeronautics Board lasted for forty years, until the agency was at last abolished. Even attempts to dismantle controls that prop up milk prices have met with repeated failure.[127]

Airline price controls were dismantled primarily because regulations had kept fares high rather than low.[128] That example reveals one of the least desirable aspects of price controls, the tendency to inhibit price competition. Some recent proposals on pharmaceuticals would do the same thing by requiring manufacturers to match discounts given to some buyers, such as Medicaid, when selling to other buyers, such as pharmacies. That requirement would remove the incentive to offer discounts in the first place. By making pricing strategy more easily observed by competitors (because government prices are a matter of public record), the rule would also remove much of the incentive to price aggressively. The Government Accounting Office recently noted that the law requiring sellers to grant Medicaid the best price offered to managed care firms effectively raised managed care prices rather than lowered Medicaid prices.[129] Nations with pervasive price controls on pharmaceuticals often spend far more of their health care budgets on pharmaceuticals than the United States (recall figure 3).

The Inability of Price Controls to Handle Complex Market Activities. Additional problems with price controls are even less obvious. Price control regimes for pharmaceuticals usually attempt to set higher prices for more innovative drugs (as in Canada, France, and elsewhere.)[130] That action requires price controllers to outguess the market in deciding which research areas are most promising and which new types of drugs would be most useful—an impossible task. Even the FDA has found it difficult to predict which new chemical entities the medical community will later regard as breakthrough treatments. For instance, the FDA did not consider the SSRI antidepressants to be breakthrough drugs.[131]

Even for drugs on the market, additional research can be expensive, yet extremely valuable. Indeed, the benefits of new research on old drugs are perhaps the least widely appreciated facet of pharmaceutical research. Such remarkable successes as the statin-class cholesterol-reducing drugs and the clot buster tPA actually found some of their most important uses as a result of large-scale clinical trials executed by their manufacturers after the drugs were in use. These are examples of a general trend.[132] Nearly a century after its discovery and marketing, ordinary aspirin was shown to be an extraordinarily effective preventative and first-line treatment for heart attacks. Clinical trials and FDA approval for aspirin's new uses required two decades or more, however.[133] The drug was off patent, and research incentives were undermined because any benefits uncovered through clinical trials could be promoted by any other aspirin manufacturer. This illustrates both the importance of research on existing drugs and the crucial role of financial incentives to conduct such research.

The practical difficulties for a price controls regime are obvious. When government price-setters set prices on existing drugs—which are being purchased by health care providers who want to keep prices as low as possible—do those price-setters have the wisdom to take into account the costs of additional research? Perhaps these government officials would ask firms to submit formal proposals for further research, along with estimated costs and potential medical benefits, plus a request to revise prices appropriately. Such a system would be hopelessly slow and cumbersome.

Controllers are even less likely to treat pharmaceutical advertising and promotion properly. Given the popular but mistaken view that advertising raises prices with little or no offsetting benefit, price controllers can hardly be expected to set prices to permit the level of promotion necessary to provide useful information and buttress competition. Such implicit restrictions on advertising would impede the developments that advertising supports, which can include important new advances in therapies as well as the benefits of heightened competition.[134]

The Nightmare Scenario of Unintended Consequences. Such difficulties could combine to defeat the goals of advocates of price controls. Research would be curtailed or channeled into lines far less challenging than those that yielded the remarkable advances of the past two decades. Pharmaceuticals for the elderly would become a less lucrative pursuit: investments would shift to more profitable arenas. Prices would remain high, albeit not as high as for truly breakthrough products. Industry profits would be persistently comfortable, as is typical for closely regulated industries. Health care providers and payers, including Medicare and other government agencies, would be at peace with the pharmaceutical industry because price increases would be moderate and predictable. After all, the providers and payers can make just as much money or balance their budgets just as well by using old inferior drugs as they can by using new superior ones.

A disastrous equilibrium of high prices for inferior drugs and large expenditures with little innovation would result—roughly what has happened in the heavily controlled Japanese pharmaceutical market.[135] The greatest harm would be the absence of valuable therapies and treatments that would not be developed because of inadequate incentives or would not be imported because of controls over prices or difficulty in obtaining marketing approval. Those harms would be invisible to the public. The system would tend to persist, despite its destructive consequences, because pharmaceutical firms, health care providers, and health care funding agencies would have learned to live with and even benefit from a system that reliably protected profits and discouraged new entrants, while ensuring stability in prices and expenditures—at a monumental cost to patients, who gain the most from new pharmaceuticals and must therefore lose the most when those drugs fail to appear.

Potential Dangers of Medicare Reimbursement

The elderly disproportionately consume pharmaceuticals. Persons sixty-five or older constitute about 12 percent of the population but account for about 30 percent of drug expenditures.[136] Medicare reimbursement has accordingly been at the center of most discussions of pharmaceutical prices and costs. Medicare covers only the drugs used in hospitals (with a few specific additions such as for kidney dialysis). About two-thirds of Medicare recipients have some kind of prescription drug insurance, but a small proportion incur substantial or even overwhelming drug costs.[137] The lack of Medicare drug reimbursement for outpatients is often seen as anomalous in a program designed to cover medical care for the elderly. As mentioned, numerous proposals for a Medicare drug benefit are under discussion.

Including drugs in the Medicare system would involve two interrelated issues. One is coverage and reimbursement: what drugs would be covered and how much money Medicare would provide to cover them. The second is the extent of Medicare control over the prices of the drugs that it covered. Undoubtedly, federal health care reimbursement mechanisms can lead to price controls. The Medicaid program for the poor began as a simple reimbursement plan but came to include strong controls over prices: legislation passed in 1990 required pharmaceutical manufacturers to grant at least a 15 percent discount for Medicaid purchases and to match any lower prices offered to large buyers, such as managed care organizations.

The history of Medicare also demonstrates that reimbursement mechanisms and price controls tend to develop together.[138] Medicare originally involved no price controls. Indeed, in the legislative debates preceding the enactment of Medicare, proponents were as vociferous in promising that their proposal would never lead to price controls for physicians and hospitals as today's supporters of a Medicare drug benefit are in abjuring price controls for pharmaceuticals. Yet controls gradually emerged, with little planning or design. A simple change introduced by the Reagan administration to limit increases in government reimbursements for Medicare patients to the rate of inflation evolved into an extraordinarily complex schedule of fees that physicians could charge to patients (even when the fees were not being reimbursed by Medicare). The medical community widely perceives the limits as extremely low. Severe sanctions, including criminal penalties, enforce the limits.

Much the same happened to fees for hospitals, medical devices, home health services, physical therapy, and the rest of medical technology. An arrangement in which medical technology and services can be purchased only at Medicare prices leads to endless disputes, much gaming of the system, and highly uncertain prices that are often dominated by political considerations. Medicare's implementation of Diagnostic-Related Groups—a single fee is assigned for a closely related set of procedures, such as a hip replacement or treating pneumonia—led immediately to the creation of an entire industry of DRG consultants, who helped inaugurate the phenomenon of DRG creep (the tendency for providers to reassign codes so as to increase the cost of a package of services).

 Recent developments have imposed chaotic rehabilitation schedules for physical therapy, nursing care, and physician services generally.[139] Bitter disputes and intrusive legislative remedies are now endemic, as illustrated by 1997 legislation that severely restricted reimbursements and by 1999 legislation that reversed a small portion of the 1997 restrictions.[140] The medical profession, acting through the American Medical Association, is suing the federal government for billions of dollars in a dispute over payment adjustments to compensate for expected movements of patients in and out of managed care.[141] The AMA is also contemplating a suit over new guidelines on

HCFA management and evaluation guidelines and is dealing with strong reactions from its members on HCFA's new seventeen-page Medicare enrollment form.[142]

Medicare reimbursement tends to evolve into price controls. Would that pattern continue in a Medicare drug benefit plan? In theory, Medicare could offer partial reimbursement for pharmaceuticals without dictating prices—as it was originally intended to do for physicians and hospitals. But a Medicare drug plan would set budgets, presumably a separate budget for pharmaceuticals alone (ignoring cost offsets elsewhere, just as European government health care budgets tend to do). The legislators and the executive branch officials who establish the drug benefit plan would have large political stakes in those budget projections, with the laudable intention that their budgets would cover all or most pharmaceuticals needed by Medicare participants. Conflicts between such a budget and the large but unpredictable costs and benefits of future pharmaceuticals would create intense pressures to abide by budget forecasts while still permitting Medicare patients to obtain the new drugs. The resulting political environment would be strongly conducive to price controls.

The Medicare drug benefit plan outlined in 1999 by President Clinton illustrates the potential for such difficulties.[143] The White House said that it did not plan to use price controls, although in December 1999 a White House spokesman stated that the industry could expect at least a threat of price controls if it did not support the administration's plan.[144]

Nonetheless, there are reasons to expect the proposed system to lead to price controls if it becomes law. The president explicitly criticized the industry for charging prices higher than those in Canada, which strictly regulates drug prices; he also directed the Department of Health and Human Services to investigate the prices of the most-used drugs.[145] Another inducement for controls lies in a little noticed but extremely important provision in the proposed plan: after the federal government has designated a single pharmaceutical benefit management firm to negotiate prices in each region, Medicare recipients could buy drugs at the negotiated prices even after reaching the limits on government-subsidized reimbursements. Medicare prices would apply even when Medicare did not pay the bill—a system of price controls. Those controls would presumably be limited to persons covered by Medicare, but they comprise some 30 percent of the market. Intense political pressure could make the rest of the population eligible for the same prices.

Finally, there is a disjunction between budget projections for the administration's Medicare proposal and the likely realities of the pharmaceutical market. The president made clear that his plan was intended to cover virtually all pharmaceutical expenses of Medicare patients.[146] The program's description as voluntary is not entirely accurate. Heavily subsidized, the drug benefit plan would offer prices below the free market (even when an individual's Medicare insurance runs out) and would require consumers to join the plan when they entered the Medicare system or lose any chance of joining the plan later. The offer would be an almost irresistible: the administration's forecasts assume that virtually all Medicare patients would join.

The administration also assumes that the plan's limits could cover almost all drug purchases. The administration has not published expenditure estimates for its plan, but they can be inferred from premium estimates that have been made public. Total spending, including the patients' share, would start at $30 billion annually in the year 2002 and increase by 5 percent per year to roughly $31.5 billion in 2003, $33 billion in 2004, and so on.

The projections must be compared with current trends. To do so, we must know how much is now being spent on pharmaceuticals for the elderly. Surprisingly little is known. Gathering such information requires large surveys. The main source is HCFA's annual Medicare Current Beneficiary Survey, which gathers data from a panel of about 12,000 Medicare beneficiaries (most of them aged rather than disabled).[147] HCFA has formally released results only through the year 1995; those data form the basis for most discussions that cite concrete numbers for the elderly.[148] HCFA has begun work on the 1996 data and has provided its estimate of total pharmaceutical spending for the elderly for the year 1996.[149] These permit a time series for the years 1992–1996, which may be combined with data on total pharmaceutical expenditures to yield the contents of table 1.

TABLE 1

PHARMACEUTICAL EXPENDITURES FOR THE ELDERLY, 1992–1996

Year	Expenditures (billions of 1997 dollars)	Total prescription drug expenditures (%)
1992	15.9	29.9
1993	16.7	29.7
1994	17.8	29.8
1995	19.4	30.2
1996	21.1	29.9

SOURCE: Medicare Current Beneficiary Survey, HCFA.

Outpatient prescription drug expenditures for the elderly have consistently comprised about 30 percent of total expenditures. Figure 1 indicates that total expenditures were about $82 billion in 1997 and $96 billion in 1998 and continue to increase at better than 10 percent annually. Drug expenditures for the elderly were about $25 billion in 1997 and $29 billion in 1998, and they probably increased by at least 10 percent in 1999 to around $33–35 billion. Future increases are likely to be larger, given the continuing expansion in the scope of therapy. In the Medicare managed care industry—whose situation strongly resembles what a federal Medicare drug benefit would face—spending on prescription drugs is expected to increase by 18–22 percent in the year 2000, with only 4–5 percent coming from price increases and the rest from increased use of existing and new drugs.[150]

Total expenses for prescription drugs for the elderly are likely to increase from the current $33–35 billion to a minimum of $45–50 billion by the year 2002. The Clinton plan, if enacted as outlined in its July 1999 proposal, would cut pharmaceutical expenditures for the elderly by more than one-third in 2002 and even more in later years. The president emphasized that the cuts would be achieved by hiring private firms to negotiate lower prices. The administration recently suggested that it was revisiting the reimbursement limit and some other features of its plan. At the same time, however, the White House has blamed the pharmaceutical industry for unreasonable prices and has raised a threat of price controls.[151] Even a revised proposal would probably involve controls of pharmaceutical expenses at levels substantially below what current trends indicate in a relatively free market.

The government may resort to price controls to meet public expectations that its Medicare plan cover most prescription costs without premium increases. Such controls would necessarily focus on new drugs, the main source of expenditures that exceed budget forecasts. If such a plan were enacted, it would almost certainly create the same fears of price controls that caused research and development spending to drop precipitously in 1994 (recall figure 5).

6
What Congress Should Do

The third revolution in pharmaceutical research is more than a leap in science. Its power comes from combining scientific research with burgeoning market institutions that include managed care, the clinical trials industry, the computer revolution, venture capital, flexible labor markets, and innovations in advertising and marketing research. It is the combination of science and markets that is expanding drug therapy to provide new health benefits to millions of persons.

The profit motive is guiding the entire enterprise, as it should. Consumers are willing to pay for the remarkable advances being achieved, just as they are willing to pay for better cars, larger houses, more travel, new electronic gadgets, and ethnic cuisine. Appropriately, many talented and energetic individuals devote themselves to improving health.

The third pharmaceutical revolution is in its early stages—unless politics heads the revolution off. What should Congress and the state legislatures do, particularly on the contentious issues of pharmaceutical prices and

Medicare coverage? They should do three things. They should recognize some basic facts about pharmaceuticals and the revolution in pharmaceutical research. They should strive above all to avoid price controls and their immense costs, including the curtailment of the revolution itself. If Congress extends Medicare to cover pharmaceuticals, it should do so in the course of reforming the system to jettison its obsolete fee-for-service approach, which makes price controls inevitable, and it should craft a drug benefit to respect the basic economics of health insurance.

Essential Facts about Pharmaceuticals and Pharmaceutical Research

Three basic facts about pharmaceutical research are essential. First, the development of an expensive new drug that saves lives or alleviates suffering is a welcome development, not one to criticize or deplore. The opportunity to pay some $60 a month to lead a more or less normal life despite advanced arthritis, without risking injury or death from ulcers, is an important advance. This is not to say that no one will suffer a financial hardship when taking advantage of the new Cox-2 inhibitors. But a choice is better than none.

Second, competition in the pharmaceutical industry is moving faster than ever. High-tech industries provide a given level of quality or effectiveness at progressively more affordable prices. Pharmaceutical prices, adjusted for quality, rapidly decline—not each and every price in the next year, but prices on average and for most drugs. Cheaper treatments for arthritis will arrive because research is moving quickly to produce competing brands and products. The same is true for antihypertensives and cholesterol-reducing treatments to prevent heart attacks, new treatments for diabetes or osteoporosis, and other breakthroughs.

Always lurking on the sidelines is the generic pharmaceutical industry, rejuvenated by the Drug Price Competition and Patent Term Restoration Act of 1984 (the Hatch-Waxman Act). Especially vigorous in the United States among advanced economies, the generic drug industry moves quickly to bring low-price brands to market after patents expire. By 1992, 72 percent of drugs moving off patent encountered generic competition within eighteen months.[152] The proportion of physical units of pharmaceuticals accounted for by generics increased from 19 percent in 1984 to 43 percent by 1995 and 47 percent in 1998 (the data are the number of capsules and other forms of dosage, not dollar sales).[153] Much more is on the way as many of today's more expensive drugs will shortly move off patent; pharmaceuticals accounting for 25 percent of prescription drug sales in the United States will go off patent over the next four years.[154]

Third, the profit motive is the only reliable source of progress in pharmaceutical research. The search for profits brought us the remarkable new drugs of the past decade and filled the research pipeline with many more. The extraordinarily difficult task of exploiting high technology to create practical solutions to difficult problems cannot be performed or supervised by governments or nonprofit agencies.

Profits tend to provoke criticism, much of it misconceived. It makes little sense to criticize people for making money by creating new cures. Not long ago the *Wall Street Journal* reported about a mathematics professor who stood to gain some $200 million from an initial public offering for an Internet startup company that planned to use his algorithm for faster downloading of web pages. The professor would become rich because someone planned to charge a lot of money for his invention. What if the same person made the same windfall profit from an invention that facilitated a better cancer cure instead of faster web access? Would such a thing be worse for society, something that deserved political attack for making money on the backs of the elderly? Should we worry about how much profit might arise from the recent Monsanto-Pharmacia merger plan (involving the intellectual resources that brought Celebrex to the market among other accomplishments), when the total market capitalization of this major new pharmaceutical firm was less than half that of the Internet search engine and portal Yahoo!?[155]

Avoid Price Controls

Government price controls are best understood as a process, one that can be as dynamic and unpredictable as pharmaceutical research itself. Price controls are invariably established with the best of intentions, usually to achieve limited goals for a limited time. Then the controls themselves go to work to create an intractable mix of vested interests and subtle market adjustments, often with the greatest harms all but invisible to outsiders. That price controls discourage investment is one of the truisms of economics. That the costs of controls fall mainly in the future is an implication of that truism.

Particularly for pharmaceuticals, however, with their bright future, price controls could do even more harm than usual. The brightness of that future lies not just in scientific progress, remarkable as it is, but in advances in market organizations that continue to astonish every day. Left alone, the market will continue to harness those advances in the interests of better health, especially for the elderly. Price controls or the threat of controls could deflect those market forces away from health to the pursuit of other goals, which may be useful in their own right but would be poor substitutes for longer and healthier lives.

Advocates of outright controls over pharmaceutical prices are only a small minority, despite the obvious temptation of populist political appeals. The real threat today comes from backdoor controls that enter through government programs with the purpose of supporting the purchase and provision of pharmaceuticals, as through the Medicare program.

How to Approach a Medicare Drug Benefit
Adding a drug benefit to the current Medicare system would be extremely dangerous. The current system is a predominantly unlimited fee-for-service arrangement wherein the government simply pays the bills as they come in—an anachronistic approach left over from the way health care markets worked when Medicare was passed in 1965. But any products and services comprehended by its fee-for-service arrangement eventually are covered by comprehensive price controls. Indeed, the system provides no way to control costs except through some combination of price controls, reimbursement limits, and queues. Price controls are always a cornerstone of such an arrangement, as evident in the Canadian and other single-payer systems.

The fee-for-service entitlement cannot be sustained. Many Medicare reform proposals explicitly advocate an end to Medicare's uncapped fee-for-service plan, replaced by something along the lines of contemporary health care markets, which are dominated by various forms of managed care.[156] The recent work of the Breaux-Thomas Commission on Medicare Reform provides an excellent example. A majority of the commission recommended that Medicare allocate funds to support individual health plan premiums (presumably adjusted for age and medical condition).[157] Participants would pay only about 12 percent of the costs and could freely choose among competing plans. The plans, which Medicare authorities would have to approve, could include fee-for-service as well as managed care. Drug benefits would be offered as part of a package or as separate plans.

Two crucial questions would arise in this or any other Medicare reform. One, would the plan permit or encourage price controls on pharmaceuticals? The adverse consequences of price controls are so great that leaving pharmaceuticals out of Medicare altogether would be better if the alternative included setting prices. A Medicare drug plan would have to be designed so as not to invite the progressive implementation of price controls, a fate that has met all other health care activities funded by Medicare. The Breaux-Thomas recommendations, which would provide defined contributions for health care plans but would not specify prices, presumably would not involve price controls. But what factors would enter the Medicare process for approving health care plans? The theoretical power to specify prices can easily evolve into a mechanism for price controls.

A second, equally important question about any Medicare reform is whether the elderly would be free to purchase medical services, including pharmaceuticals, outside their plan's limits. If they could, market incentives would continue to yield pharmaceutical advances. But if Medicare patients could not purchase pharmaceuticals outside the system—just as they now cannot purchase nonreimbursed medical care except under onerous conditions—the effect would be to create de facto price controls.

If Congress does create a Medicare drug benefit, it should respect the basic economics of insurance. One of those principles is that insurance should not cover events that involve little or no financial risk. Here we must note the emerging role of pharmaceuticals for the elderly. Many people today can expect to lead relatively healthy and enjoyable lives through their eighties and perhaps into their nineties. In doing so, they will almost certainly make liberal use of pharmaceuticals, which are now attacking the most common illnesses and disabilities of old age and advanced age. It makes sense for consumers to prepare for a lengthy retirement that includes pharmaceuticals along with recreation, travel, special living arrangements, good dining, and all the other products and services that are already finding huge new markets among the elderly who are healthy. There is no individual or social benefit to selecting one component of these expected expenses—pharmaceuticals—and processing it through an insurance system, with its attendant administrative costs and debates over "health" compared with "lifestyle" pharmaceuticals.

A related principle from the economics of insurance concerns financial limits. Deductibles should be substantial. Passing all pharmaceutical purchases through insurance, instead of only those exceeding, say, $500–1,000 per year, would create unnecessary administrative costs and would remove incentives for reasonably careful use of pharmaceuticals. Conversely, insurance should provide coverage for catastrophic costs, with limits on out-ofpocket costs. All of this should be means tested so as to provide a safety net for the impoverished elderly.[158]

Private insurance is invariably more efficient and less susceptible to political manipulation than insurance provided by the government. A voucher system, which is essentially what the Breaux-Thomas Commission recommended, would be far superior to an insurance plan run directly by Medicare. The special problems of bringing pharmaceuticals into the Medicare fold—along with the simple fact that doing so involves new legislation and a new administrative mechanism—suggests that something akin to Breaux-Thomas might be adopted for pharmaceuticals even if the rest of Medicare were left untouched. That action would, among other things, provide important new evidence to inform the larger debate over Medicare reform.

Even such a modest system would be far from foolproof. It would be difficult to solve the problem of adverse selection. (That is the tendency for those most likely to need expensive treatments to choose the most generous insurance plan and thus drive up costs and premiums; the less-sick opt for leaner plans and thus push costs up further. Eventually premiums can climb so high that insurance plans for sicker participants provide little financial benefit.) Also, a catastrophe benefit could raise difficult problems in deciding which new therapies (offered with the expectation of full government coverage) would be worth their cost. Nonetheless, a market-oriented Medicare reform could permit the pharmaceutical revolution to continue.

Notes

Chapter 1
Introduction

1. These controversies were discussed in the following recent articles by Robert Pear: "New England Lawmakers Consider Drug Strategies," *New York Times,* December 17, 1999, and "Clinton Officials Warn Drug Firms of Price Controls," *New York Times,* December 25, 1999.

2. A prominent proposal for federal legislation is the Allen bill (H.R. 664), which would require pharmaceutical firms to offer pharmacies the same discounts granted to the federal government. See Tim Johnson and Tom Allen, "The Prescriptions or the Rent? How to End Biased Drug Pricing against the Uninsured Elderly," *Washington Post,* August 3, 1999. Recently a group of New England legislators publicly explored a variety of measures, including direct price controls. See Carey Goldberg, "New England Lawmakers Consider Drug Strategies," *New York Times,* December 17, 1999.

3. A convenient summary of leading proposals for a Medicare drug benefit if offered in Henry J. Kaiser Family Foundation 1999. I discuss the Clinton plan in chapter 5.

4. Again, see Pear, "Clinton Officials."

Chapter 2
Spending More on Pharmaceuticals

5. Barents Group 1999, i, cites data from the Health Care Financing Administration in the Department of Health and Human Services and, for 1998, data from the Scott-Levin Source Prescription Audit.

6. HCFA 1999.

7. IMS Health, *Drug Monitor,* December 1998, August 1999, and September 1999.

8. OECD 1999.

9. See HIAA 1999. Figures 1 and 2 show that drug prices have increased at less than 4 percent annually .

10. Ibid. Figures 1 and 2 also show that drug expenditures have increased in double digits. See also PhRMA 1999, figure 4–11, 49, which breaks down the increased expenditures for prescription drugs in comparisons of price, volume, and so forth and shows that price increases accounted for about one-fifth of the increases in such expenditures in 1997 and 1998. The data come from IMS Health 1999b.

11. Triplett 1999, especially chapter 3.

12. The 1997 and 1998 data come from IMS Health. Of the innovative Celebrex and Vioxx, Celebrex, introduced early in 1999, generated more revenues in its first year than any previous drug; see Robert Langreth and Thomas M. Burto, "Merck's Vioxx Is Gaining on Rival Product Celebrex," *Wall Street Journal,* November 24, 1999. IMS data indicate a 4 percent decline in non-narcotic analgesics between 1997 and 1998, that is, before the arrival of Celebrex. A report from a pharmaceutical benefit management firm indicates that managed care organizations' per patient spending on nonsteroidal antiinflammatory drugs (NSAIDs) by increased by less than 4 percent between 1997 and 1998, but much more spending was expected in 1999 with the arrival of the Cox-2 inhibitors; see Teitelbaum et al. 1999, 39, 53.

13. Vakil 1996.

14. Fagan et al. 1998.

15. *Hospital and Community Psychiatry 1990.* An analysis from a Canadian government agency, reaching similar conclusion, comes from Glennie 1997.

16. On depression, see Frank et al. 1999. On congestive heart failure, see "Provide Education about Congestive Heart Failure and Pump Up Your Savings," *Managed Healthcare* 8 (4) (April 1998): 42–44, and SOLVD 1999. On strokes, see Fagan et al. 1998; Secondary and Tertiary Prevention 1996. On migraine headaches, see Legg et al. 1997a, b. On kidney disease, see Levy 1993 and Showstack et al. 1989.

17. On recent Medicare spending, see Robert Pear, "Yearly Medicare Spending Drops for First Time, in Fiscal '99," *New York Times,* November 13, 1999. I am unaware of a systematic analysis of these parallel trends.

18. Hu et al. 1999.

19. Legg et al. 1997b.

20. On antidepressants, see Berndt et al. 1998. On kidney disease, see Levy 1993.

21. A recent summary of progress against heart disease is reported by the Center for Disease Control in "Decline in Deaths from Heart Disease and Stroke—United States, 1900–1999," *Morbidity and Mortality Weekly Report,* August 6, 1999. On the impact of medical treatments, see Cutler, McClellan, and Newhouse 1999, especially their description of the forthcoming study by Heidenreich and McClelland.

22. On treating heart attacks during the 1980s and early 1990s, see Cutler et al. 1998 and Cutler, McClellan, and Newhouse 1999. But, as noted, hospital costs for the elderly have unexpectedly declined in the past few years even as pharmaceutical costs for heart disease continued to mount.

23. Richmond 1999 offers a useful overview of the influence of genomics (one area in which science is advancing especially rapidly).

24. See Tufts 1999a.

25. See Tufts 1999b.

26. On the increasing cost and complexity of FDA-mandated clinical trials, see DiMasi 1995 and Grabowski and Vernon 2000.

27. Fascinating details on the clinical trials industry (albeit with a focus on individual episodes involving questionable ethics) are reported in three *New York Times* stories: "Cost-Cutting Forges New Drug-Testing Industry," May 16, 1999; Kurt Eichenwald and Gina Kolata, "Drug Trials Hide Conflicts for Doctors," May 16, 1999; and Eichenwald and Kolata, "Research for Hire: A Doctor's Drug Studies Turn into Fraud," May 17, 1999. An American Medical Association newsletter published a more positive article that encouraged physicians to participate in this process; see Alison Miller, "Trial Run: Small Practices Can Participate in Clinical Trials: Here's How," *American Medical News*, September 27, 1999. On the enhanced role of practicing physicians and their patients, see also "Commentary: The War against Cancer Needs New Recruits," *Business Week*, May 31, 1999.

28. See Miller, "Trial Run."

29. Calfee 1996 reviews the off-label uses and the tensions between the FDA and physicians regarding the restrictions on off-label information. In a joint American Enterprise Institute–American Cancer Society survey of oncologists in 1997, 91 percent of respondents agreed that patient care would be adversely restricted if physicians were to use drugs only as indicated on FDA labels (Calfee and McGinniss 1997).

30. Aside from the FDA approval process, pharmaceutical firms face strong market incentives to avoid introducing unsafe drugs. See, for example, Peltzman 1973, 1987.

31. Friedman et al. 1999.

32. David Woodruff, "Only in France; Government Is Fining Companies That Let People Work Late," *Wall Street Journal*, June 10, 1999.

33. Kevin J. Delaney and David Wessel, "Stock Options Fail to Catch On in Much of High-Tech Europe," *Wall Street Journal*, December 21, 1999.

Chapter 3
More Than Expected

34. Citations on such developments are readily available in leading medical journals (especially useful are the periodic review articles on "drug therapy" in the *New England Journal of Medicine*).

35. On the origins of Cox-2 inhibitors, see Calfee 1999, also available in a slightly expanded version at www.aei.org. When the FDA approved Celebrex

(and later Vioxx) for marketing, it did not approve any claims for superiority of Cox-2 inhibitors in avoiding ulcers. But recent research has found, as expected, that the Cox-2 inhibitors significantly reduced stomach ulcers; in the case of rheumatoid arthritis, ulcer rates were only one-fourth those of NSAIDs (traditional nonsteroidal antiinflammatory drugs such as aspirin) and hardly greater than with treatment with a placebo. See Simon et al. 1999 and the accompanying editorial by Peterson and Cryer 1999.

36. Robert Langreth and Thomas M. Burto, "Merck's Vioxx Is Gaining on Rival Product Celebrex," *Wall Street Journal*, November 24, 1999.

37. See Gorman 1997 and Preston, O'Neal, and Talaga 1994.

38. Reissman 1998 and Ellickson, Stern, and Trajtenberg 1999.

39. On compliance problems in using antidepressants, see Melfi et al. 1998.

40. See Raju Narisetti, "P&G Applies Packaging Savvy to Its New Prescription Drug," *Wall Street Journal*, January 30, 1997.

41. The examples in the text are taken from Kettler 1998, 41, citing data from Morgan Stanley Dean Witter 1998. The data are reproduced in PhRMA 1999, 59.

42. See Langreth and Burto, "Merck's Vioxx." On pricing, see David J. Morrow, "Monsanto and Merck Pushing New Arthritis Drugs," *New York Times,* August 3, 1999.

43. On price competition among antidepressants, see "Bitter Medicine Ahead for Drug Companies," *Business Week*, May 3, 1999. A review of a book by D. John Betteridge conveniently summarizes the development of the statin drugs (Katan 1997).

44. See Anne Fawcett, "Actos Provides Diabetes Patients Another Alternative to Rezulin," *Wall Street Journal*, July 19, 1999.

45. "Bitter Medicine Ahead," *Business Week.*

46. Ron Winslow, "Stroke Drug May Extend 'Window' for Treatment," *Wall Street Journal*, February 5, 1999.

47. Barents Group 1999, 15–19. See also Laurie McGinley, "Heavy Advertising Is Cited in Rapid Rise of Drug Costs," *Wall Street Journal*, July 7, 1999.

48. Kettler 1998, 40–46.

49. On adjusting price indexes for quality, see Triplett 1999; chapter 3, about the prices of antidepressants, is of special relevance.

50. This section is based on Calfee 2000.

51. The figures are in 1995 dollars. OECD 1999.

52. Citations on these point are readily available in leading medical journals. On the ability of lipid-lowering drugs to prevent angioplasty, see Pitt et al. 1999.

53. On the redefined health risks of obesity, see Lean et al. 1999. On lipid-reducing drugs, see later citations on statin drugs. For the 75 percent at-risk figure for four conditions, see Schwartz and Woloshin 1999.

54. David Brown, "Medicine's Growth Curve: Healthy Patients As Doctors Treat Risk as a Disease, Cost-Benefit Issues Arise," *Washington Post*, October 22, 1999.

55. See Robert A. Rosenblatt, "Drug Firms' TV Ads Fuel Rise in Costs and Demand," *Los Angeles Times*, November 26, 1999. See also HIAA 1999 and Hollan 1999. A late 1997 poll of physicians found a strong majority desiring that direct-to-consumer advertising for prescription drugs be reduced or eliminated (IMS Health 1997).

56. This history is briefly recounted in FDA 1999, published two years after the policy change that permitted broadcast advertising of prescription drugs without including the notoriously detailed "brief summary" of medical matters that must accompany all print advertising of prescription drugs.

57. Simoons and Casparie 1999.

58. *American Medical News*, December 27, 1999.

59. On depression, see "Depression Seriously Undertreated," *AMA Science News Update*, January 29, 1997, describing the conclusions of a consensus panel of the National Depressive and Manic Depressive Association. On diabetes, see Leape 1995. On asthma, the National Heart, Lung and Blood Institute declared in 1997 the illness underdiagnosed and undertreated (Sally Squires, "Asthma Treatment Should Be Prompt, Federal Panel Says," *Washington Post*, February 25, 1997). On osteoporosis, the findings of the National Osteoporosis Risk Assessment Study are described by Jane E. Allen, "A Feeling Deep in Your Bones," *Los Angeles Times*, February 22, 1999. On serum cholesterol, see Cleeman and Lenfant 1998 and "Cholesterol-Cutting Drugs Go Unused," *New York Times*, March 9, 1999, based on a recent meeting of the American College of Cardiology. On hypertension, see Berlowitz et al. 1998.

60. Again, see Brown, "Medicine's Growth Curve."

61. This argument is reviewed in detail in Calfee 1997, chapter 2. On health claims for foods, see Calfee and Pappalardo 1991 and Ippolito and Mathios 1991.

62. See Kane and Garrard 1994. A recent review of numerous surveys of physicians concluded that about 10 percent of physicians are unaware of relevant practice guidelines and a larger proportion fail to follow the guidelines for various reasons (Cabana et al. 1999). Again see Miller, "Trial Run."

63. The drug is Ramipril; see Heart Outcomes Prevention Evaluation Study Investigators 1999. The study was halted and its results released early because of the drug's strong effects in preventing mortality.

64. The ad was for Zoloft.

65. *New York Times*, "Cholesterol-Cutting Drugs Go Unused," March 9, 1999. On the underuse of aspirin and beta-blockers as well as cholesterol-reducing drugs for patients who have had heart attacks, see McCormick et al. 1999.

66. Morrow, "Monsanto and Merck."

67. Barents 1999, 14–15.

68. Ramsay et al. 1999.

69. Kohlmeier 1990.

70. Kane and Garrard 1994.

71. On hypertension, see Ramsay et al. 1999. On osteoporosis, see Kohlmeier 1999.

72. See Masson and Rubin 1985; also see Calfee 1997, chapter 2.

73. GAO 1999.

74. IMS Health 1999.

75. Barents Group 1999, 5.

76. From the AMA's *Science News Update*, January 29, 1997, released shortly after the FDA approved tPA for strokes.

77. The preceding details are also from *Science News Update*, January 29, 1997.

78. *New York Times*, May 2, 1997, and other newspapers. The ads were run by Genentech, the manufacturer of tPA.

79. "Pushing Ethical Pharmaceuticals Direct to the Public," *Lancet*, March 28, 1998, p. 351.

80. Calfee 1997, chap. 9

81. It is widely believed that the Viagra ads have increased the number of men seeking medical attention for erectile dysfunction.

82. Robert Langreth, "Drug Marketing Drives Many Clinical Trials," *Wall Street Journal*, November 16, 1998, describes research by Bristol-Myers Squibb for its Prevachol brand. The study was published in Shephard et al. 1995.

83. Ross et al. 1999.

84. Moore 1989a, 1989b, 1993.

85. The data on clinical trials came from Langreth, "Drug Marketing." On the advertising agency acquisition, see Kathryn Kranhold, "Lowe Group Sets Deal to Aid Drug Marketing," *Wall Street Journal*, November 9, 1999.

Chapter 4
The Budgeting Problem

86. In addition to earlier citations, see Barents Group 1999.

87. Ross et al. 1999.

88. See Laura Johannes, "Tailor-Made Cancer Vaccines Show Promise in Early Trials," *Wall Street Journal*, November 18, 1999.

89. See Gina Kolata, "The Fat War; Hope amid the Harm," *New York Times,* October 31, 1999, which notes that research continues even though initial clinical trials were a disappointment when leptin was simply used as a drug.

90. Robert Langreth, "Drug Firms Are Making Progress in an Effort to Slow Alzheimer's," *Wall Street Journal*, October 22, 1999.

91. Nemeroff 1998.

Chapter 5
The Threat of Price Controls

92. For example, Carey Goldberg, "New England Lawmakers Consider Drug Strategies," *New York Times,* December 17, 1999, and Pear, "Clinton Officials Warn Drug Firms." A January 1, 2000, *New York Times* story reported that a spokesman for the vice president "said that Mr. Gore had consistently opposed [the pharmaceutical industry's] interests by supporting price controls on prescription drugs."

93. See Clarkson 1996. Also see PhRMA 1999, 24, citing the work of Frederick Scherer.

94. See Grabowski and Vernon 1994, 2000.

95. This history is described in Helms 1999.

96. IM Health data, cited in PhRMA 1999.

97. See, for example, Marc Kaufman, "Pricey Pills," *Washington Post,* November 9, 1999.

98. Danzon 1997, 1999.

99. Ibid.

100. This section also draws on Calfee 2000.

101. Again, see Lean et al. 1999; see also Thompson et al. 1999.

102. Williamson 1999. Also, much of the October 27, 1999, *Journal of the American Medical Association* was devoted to obesity, including the topics discussed here.

103. See Serdula et al. 1999.

104. The failure of antismoking advice to reduce heart disease mortality from smoking is documented in Ebrahim and Smith 1997. Pharmaceutical treatments include nicotine replacement (chewing gum, patches, and inhalers) and antidepressants; see Hajek et al. 1999.

105. On patches, see the useful August 17, 1999, *New York Times* article, "Challenge of Patch Drugs; Getting under the Skin." On ovaries and cancer therapy, see *New York Times*, October 26, 1999, "Experiment Seeks to Protect Ovaries from Cancer Treatment." On the search for substitutes for insulin injections, see Robert Langreth, "Merck Discovery May Lead to Helpful Pills for Diabetics," *Wall Street Journal*, May 7, 1999, containing the "godsend" quotation from the ADA president.

106. On measuring consumer valuations of the prevention of pain and suffering, see Calfee and Winston 1993.

107. On the ability of patches to improve compliance, see, again, Langreth, "Merck Discovery." On antidepressants and compliance, see Peveler et al. 1999.

108. *Wall Street Journal*, January 25 and August 13, 1999.

109. The March 29, 1999, issue of *Business Week* offers a useful and thorough discussion of both successes and failures in research on diabetes.

110. Genentech is another firm that has yet to find success in this pursuit; see Ralph T. King Jr., "Genentech's Heart-Disease Drug Fails to Show Clear Benefit in Test Patients," *Wall Street Journal*, February 19, 1999.

111. A death that was almost certainly caused by experimental gene therapy aroused substantial controversy in December 1999 even as it highlighted the potential benefits of this approach; see Rick Weiss and Deborah Nelson, "Death Raises Questions of Ethics, Profit, Science," *Washington Post*, December 31, 1999.

112. See Lynch 1992.

113. On biochips, see American College of Surgeons 1999. See also *Economist*, October 23, 1999, "New Chips Off the Block."

114. On the Clinton health plan and its implications for the pharmaceutical industry, see Grabowski 1994.

115. Stephen D. Moore, "Hopes Dwindle That EU Will Dismantle Draconian Price Controls on Medicines," *Wall Street Journal*, December 7, 1998.

116. On diabetes and nerve damage and its consequences, see *Business Week*, March 29, 1999, "New Weapons to Cut Diabetes' Toll."

117. On developments in the next generation of antidepressants, see *New York Times*, October 18, 1999.

118. Elizabeth Olson, "Drug Groups and U.N. Offices Join to Develop Malaria Cures," *New York Times*, November 18, 1999.

119. See FDA 1996, noting that 131 orphan drugs had been approved since the Orphan Drug Act passed in 1982.

120. *Economist*, "Balms for the Poor," August 14, 1999, discusses recent events in connection with treatments for malaria and other tropical diseases.

121. Ibid.

122. Butler 1993, 3–21.

123. Danzon 1997, 1999.

124. On Japan, see Thomas 1994a; on France, see Thomas 1994b and Danzon 1997.

125. Tierney 1998.

126. Based on the author's personal experience while living in Massachusetts, where insurance firms are prohibited from discounting below prices specified by the commonwealth of Massachusetts.

127. Michael M. Weinstein, "Efforts to Change Milk Price Rules Fizzle," *New York Times Magazine*, April 11, 1999.

128. Morrison and Winston 1995.

129. GAO 1999.

130. Kettler 1998, 10; Danzon 1997.

131. Goldberg 1995.

132. Kettler 1998, 46–48.

133. For the history of this drug, particularly the battle to demonstrate and then gain FDA approval for its effects on heart disease, see Mann and Plummer 1991. A recent update is Hennekens 1997.

134. There is compelling evidence that advertising tends to reduce prices even when the advertising does not itself focus on price; see Calfee 1997, chapter 4.

135. Thomas 1994a.

136. The July 22, 1999, analysis by the White House's National Economic Council (p. 3) states these proportions as 12 percent and one-third, respectively; see Office of the President 1999. As described below, surprisingly little is known about total pharmaceutical expenditures by or for the elderly, but the best estimates consistently suggest elderly expenditures exceeding 30 percent of total expenditures; see table 1.

137. Davis et al. 1999.

138. On the evolution of Medicare reimbursement from a fee-for-service arrangement into a full-fledged price controls system with draconian controls, see Hoff 1998.

139. In 1998, Medicare initiated a policy of prohibiting physicians from providing any non-Medicare–approved services to Medicare patients. The policy has been subjected to intense criticism and tested by litigation. The Department of Health and Human Services has apparently relaxed the most draconian of its provisions, a prohibition on patients obtaining any nonreimbursed services from physicians who treat Medicare patients. On the drastic fluctuations in Medicare reimbursement for home health care, a result of intrusive legislation, see David S. Hilzenrath, "Patients Face a Limit on Benefits for Therapy," *Washington Post*, May 10, 1999.

140. See, for example, Carol Gentry, "Unintended Consequence Causes Medicare Outcry," *Wall Street Journal*, November 16, 1999.

141. "AMA Suit; Medicare Underpaid $3.2 Billion," *American Medical News*, December 20, 1999.

142. "Medicare Enrollment Form Overwhelms Delegates," *American Medical News*, December 27, 1999, and "HCFA Lags on E&M Issue; Doctors Contemplate Legal Action," *American Medical News*, December 27, 1999.

143. The July 22, 1999, analysis by the White House's National Economic Council is the source for the description of the clinical proposal provided here.

144. Robert Pear, "Clinton Will Seek a Medicare Change on Drug Coverage," *New York Times*, June 8, 1999. The story quotes a high-ranking official: "We would never do price controls." Pear, "Clinton Officials Warn Drug Firms," describes the threat of controls.

145. James Gerstenzan, "Clinton Scolds Drug Industry on High Costs for Elderly," *Los Angeles Times*, October 26, 1999.

146. Office of the President 1999.

147. This survey is described by former and current HCFA staff members in Davis et al. 1999.

148. See ibid. for an analysis of much of the 1995 data.

149. HCFA 1999.

150. "Tufts Alters Drug Benefit Design to Slow Drivers of Pharmaceutical Costs," *BNA Health Care Policy Report*, September 27, 1999, p. 1528–29.

151. Again, see Pear, "Clinton Officials Warn."

Chapter 6
What Congress Should Do

152. Grabowski and Vernon 1995.

153. Data from IMS Health, cited in PhRMA 1999, 61.

154. *Business Week*, November 30, 1998, "New Teeth for Old Patents."

155. On January 12, 2000, Yahoo! had a market capitalization of approximately $100 billion, while Pharmacia-Upjohns' capitalization was $24.6 billion and Monsanto's, $22.5 billion.

156. Helms 1999 covers many issues in Medicare reform.

157. Ten of the seventeen members of the commission approved the Breaux-Thomas proposal, but that count was one vote short of the eleven votes required for a formal recommendation.

158. See the analysis in Pauly 1999.

References

American College of Surgeons. 1999. Press release regarding Sarkis Meterissian, "Biochip Technology Opens the Door for Researchers to Tailor Chemotherapy to the Genetic Makeup of a Tumor." San Francisco Convention, October.

Barents Group Llc. 1999. "Factors Affecting the Growth of Prescription Drug Expenditures." Report prepared for the National Institute for Health Care Management Research and Educational Foundation. Washington, D.C. July.

Berlowitz, Dan R., Arlene S. Ash, Elaine C. Hickey, Robert H. Friedman, Mark Glickman, and Boris Kader. 1998. "Inadequate Management of Blood Pressure in a Hypertensive Population." *New England Journal of Medicine* 339 (27) (December 31): 1957–63.

Berndt, Ernest, Sean Finkelstein, Paul Greenberg, Robert H. Howland, Alison Keith, A. John Rush, James Russell, and Martin Keller. 1998. "Workplace Performance Effects from Chronic Depression and Its Treatment." *Journal of Health Economics* 17 (5): 511–35.

Butler, Stuart M. 1993. "The Fatal Attraction of Price Controls." In *Health Policy Reform: Competition and Controls,* edited by Robert B. Helms. Washington, D.C.: AEI Press.

Cabana, Michael D., Cynthia S. Rand, Neil R. Powe, Albert W. Wu, Modena H. Wilson, Paul-André C. Abboud, and Haya R. Rubin. 1999. "Why Don't Physicians Follow Clinical Practice Guidelines? A Framework for Improvement." *Journal of the American Medical Association* 282 (15) (October 20): 1458–65.

Calfee, John E. 1996. "The Leverage Principle in FDA Regulation of Information." In *Competitive Strategies in the Pharmaceutical Industry,* edited by Robert Helms. Washington, D.C.: AEI Press.

—————. 1997. *Fear of Persuasion: A New Perspective on Advertising and Regulation.* London: Agora.

——————. 1999. "Price Controls Are a Prescription for Disaster." *Wall Street Journal*, July 22.

——————. 2000. "The Increasing Necessity for Market-Based Pharmaceutical Prices." *Pharmacoeconomics*.

Calfee, John E., and Lamar McGinniss. 1997. "A Representative National Survey of Oncologists on Off-Label Prescribing and FDA Policies toward Information Dissemination." American Enterprise Institute.

Calfee, John E., and Janis K. Pappalardo. 1991. "Public Policy Issues in Health Claims for Foods." *Journal of Public Policy and Marketing* 10 (1) (spring): 33–54.

Calfee, John E., and Clifford Winston. 1993. "The Consumer Welfare Effects of Liability for Pain and Suffering: An Exploratory Analysis." *Brookings Papers on Economic Activity: Microeconomics* 1: 133–74.

Clarkson, Kenneth W. 1996. "The Effects of Research and Promotion on Rates of Return." In *Competitive Strategies in the Pharmaceutical Industry*, edited by Robert Helms. Washington, D.C.: AEI Press.

Cleeman, James I., and Claude Lenfant. 1998. "The National Cholesterol Education Program: Progress and Prospects." *Journal of the American Medical Association* 280 (December 23): 2099–2104.

Cutler, David, Mark McClellan, and Joseph Newhouse. 1999. "The Costs and Benefits of Intensive Treatment for Cardiovascular Disease." In *Measuring the Prices of Medical Treatments*, edited by Jack Triplett. Washington, D.C.: Brookings Institution.

Cutler, David, Mark McClellan, Joseph Newhouse, and D. Remler. 1998 "Are Medical Prices Declining? Evidence for Heart Attack Treatments." *Quarterly Journal of Economics* 113 (4): 991–1024.

Danzon, Patricia M. 1997. *Pharmaceutical Price Regulation: National Policies versus Global Interests*. Washington, D.C.: AEI Press.

——————. 1999. *Price Comparisons for Pharmaceuticals: A Review of U.S. and Cross-National Studies*. Washington, D.C.: AEI Press.

Davis, Margaret, John Poisal, George Chulis, Carlos Zarabozo, and Barbara Cooper. 1999. "Prescription Drug Coverage, Utilization, and Spending among Medicare Beneficiaries." *Health Affairs* 18 (1) (January–February): 231–43.

DiMasi, Joseph A. 1995. "Trends in Drug Development Costs, Times, Risks." *Drug Information Journal* 29 (2): 375–84.

Ebrahim, Shah, and George Davey Smith. 1997. "Systematic Review of Randomized Controlled Trials of Multiple Risk Factor Interventions for Preventing Coronary Heart Disease." *British Medical Journal* 314 (June 7):1666.

Ellickson, Paul, Scott Stern, and Manuel Trajtenberg. 1999. "Patient Welfare and Patient Compliance: An Empirical Framework for Measuring the Benefits from Pharmaceutical Innovation." National Bureau of Economic Research Working Paper 6890. NBER.

Fagan, S. C., L. B. Morgenstern, A. Petitta, R. E. Ward, B. C. Tilley, J. R. Marler, S. R. Levine, J. P. Broderick, T. G. Kwiatkowski, M. Frankel, T. G.

Brott, and M. D. Walker. 1998. "Cost-Effectiveness of Tissue Plasminogen Activator for Acute Ischemic Stroke." *Neurology* 5 (50): 883–89.

Food and Drug Administration. 1996. Statement by Michael Friedman, deputy commissioner for operations, Subcommittee on Human Resources and Intergovernmental Relations, Committee on Government Reform and Oversight, U.S. House of Representatives, September 12.

——————. 1999. "Guidance for Industry: Consumer-Directed Broadcast Advertisements." Washington, D.C.: Government Printing Office.

Frank, Richard G., et al. 1999. "Price Indexes for the Treatment of Depression." In *Measuring the Prices of Medical Treatments,* edited by Jack Triplett. Washington, D.C.: Brookings Institution.

Friedman, Michael A., Janet Woodcock, Murray M. Lumpkin, Jeffrey E. Shuren, Arthur E. Hass, and Larry J. Thompson. 1999. "The Safety of Newly Approved Medicines: Do Recent Market Removals Mean There Is a Problem?" *Journal of the American Medical Association* 28 (May 12):11728–34.

Glennie, Judith L. 1997. "Pharmacoeconomic Evaluations of Clozapine in Treatment-Resistant Schizophrenia and Risperidone in Chronic Schizophrenia." *Technology Overview: Pharmaceuticals* 7.0 (July).

Goldberg, Robert M. 1995. "Breaking up the FDA's Medical Information Monopoly." *Regulation* 18 (2): 40–52.

Gorman, Jack M. 1997. *The Essential Guide to Psychiatric Drugs.* 3rd ed. New York: St. Martin's.

Grabowski, Henry G. 1994. *Health Reform and Pharmaceutical Innovation.* Washington, D.C.: AEI Press, 1994.

Grabowski, Henry G., and John Vernon. 1994. "Returns to Research and Development on New Drug Introductions in the 1980s." *Journal of Health Economics* 13: 383–406.

——————. 1995. "Longer Patents for Increased Generic Competition: The Waxman-Hatch Act after One Decade." Working paper.

——————. 2000. "New Findings on the Returns to Pharmaceutical Research and Development." *Pharmacoeconomics.*

Hajek, Peter, Robert West, Jonathan Foulds, Fredrik Nilsson, Sylvia Burrows, and Anna Meadow. 1999. "Randomized Comparative Trial of Nicotine Polacrilex, a Transdermal Patch, Nasal Spray, and an Inhaler." *Archives of Internal Medicine* 159 (September 27): 2033–38.

Health Industry Association of America. 1999. "Prescription Drugs: Cost and Coverage Trends."

Heart Outcomes Prevention Evaluation Study Investigators. 1999. "Effects of an Angiotensin-Converting Enzyme Inhibitor, Ramipril, on Death from Cardiovascular Causes, Myocardial Infarction, and Stroke in High-Risk Patients." *New England Journal of Medicine* (November 10).

Heidenreich, Paul, and Mark McClellan. 1998. "Trends in Heart Attack Treatments and Outcomes, 1975–1995: A Literature Review and Synthesis."

References

Helms, Robert B. 1999. *Medicare in the Twenty-first Century: Seeking Fair and Efficient Reform*. Washington, D.C.: AEI Press.

——————. 1999. "The Tax Treatment of Health Insurance: Early History and Evidence, 1940–1970." In *Empowering Health Care Consumers through Tax Reform*, edited by Grace-Marie Arnett. Ann Arbor: University of Michigan Press.

Hennekens, Charles H. 1997. "Aspirin in the Treatment and Prevention of Cardiovascular Disease." *Annual Review of Public Health* 18: 37–49.

Henry J. Kaiser Family Foundation. 1999. "Prescription Drug Coverage for Medicare Beneficiaries: A Side-by-Side Comparison of Selected Proposals as of September 20, 1999." Menlo Park, Calif.: HJKFF.

Hoff, John. 1998. *Medicare Private Contracting: Paternalism or Autonomy*. Washington, D.C.: AEI Press.

Hu, X. Henry, Leona E. Markson, Richard B. Lipton, Walter F. Steward, and Marc L. Berger. 1999. "Burden of Migraine in the United States: Disability and Economic Costs." *Archives of Internal Medicine* 8 (April 26): 813–18.

IMS Health. 1997. "Majority of Physicians Want 'Direct-to-Consumer' Prescription Ads to Decrease or Disappear." Plymouth Meeting. December 2.

——————. 1998. *Drug Monitor*. December.

——————. 1999. *Drug Monitor*. August and September.

——————. 1999. *Retail and Provider Perspective*.

——————. 1999. "1999 Direct-to-Consumer Prescription Drug Advertising in U.S. Reaches $905 Million through June."

Ippolito, Pauline, and Alan Mathios. 1991. "Health Claims in Food Marketing: Evidence on Knowledge and Behavior in the Cereal Market." *Journal of Public Policy and Marketing* 10 (1) (spring): 15–32.

Kane, Robert L., and Judith Garrard. 1994. "Changing Physician Prescribing Practices: Regulation vs Education." *Journal of the American Medical Association* 271 (5): 393–94.

Katan, Martijn B. 1997. "Review of D. John Betteridge, ed., *Lipids: Current Perspectives*." *New England Journal of Medicine* 336 (19) (May 8): 1394.

Kettler, Hannah. 1998. *Competition through Innovation, Innovation through Competition*. London: Office of Health Economics.

Kohlmeier, Lynn. 1999. "Osteoporosis Update: Prevention and Treatment." *Drug Benefit Trends* 11 (7) (July): 43–44, 47–50, 53–54.

Lean, Michael E. J., Thang S. Han, and Jacob C. Seidell. 1999. "Impairment of Health and Quality of Life Using New US Federal Guidelines for the Identification of Obesity." *Archives of Internal Medicine* 159 (April 26): 159837–43.

Leape, Lucian L. 1995. "Translating Medical Science into Medical Practice: Do We Need a National Standards Board?" *Journal of the American Medical Association* 273 (19) (May 17):1535–37.

Lebowitz, B. D., J. L. Pearson, L. S. Schneider, C. F. Reynolds, G. S. Alexopoulos, M. L. Bruce, Y. Conwell, I. R. Katz, B. S. Meyers, M. F. Morrison, J. Mossey, G. Niederehe, and P. Parmelee. 1997. "Diagnosis and

Treatment of Depression in Late Life: Consensus Statement Update." *Journal of the American Medical Association* 278 (14): 1186–90.

Legg, R. F., D. A. Sclar, H. L. Nemec, J. Tarnai, and J. I. Mackowiak. 1997a. "Cost-Effectiveness of Sumatriptan in a Managed Care Population." *Journal of Managed Care* 3 (1) (January): 117–22.

————. 1997b. "Cost Benefit of Sumatriptan to an Employer." *Journal of Occupational and Environmental Medicine* 39 (7) (July): 652–57.

Levy, R. A. 1993. "What to Tell Patients about the Cost-Benefit of Medications." *Wellcome Trends in Pharmacy.*

Lynch, Michael C. 1992. *The Fog of Commerce: The Failure of Long-Term Oil Market Forecasting.* Center for International Studies, MIT.

Mann, Charles C., and Mark Plummer. 1991. *Aspirin Wars.* New York: Knopf.

Masson, Alison, and Paul Rubin. 1985. "Matching Prescription Drugs and Consumers: The Benefits of Direct Advertising." *New England Journal of Medicine* 313 (August 22): 513–15.

McCormick, Danny, Jerry H. Gurwitz, Darleen Lessard, Yorge Yarzebski, Joel M. Gore, and Robert J. Goldberg. 1999. "Use of Aspirin, Beta-Blockers, and Lipid-Lowering Medications before Recurrent Acute Myocardial Infarction: Missed Opportunities for Prevention?" *Archives of Internal Medicine* 159 (March 22): 561–67.

Melfi, Catherine A., Anita J. Chawla, Thomas W. Croghan, Mark P. Hanna, Sean Kennedy, and Kate Sredl. 1998. "The Effects of Adherence to Antidepressant Treatment Guidelines on Relapse and Recurrence of Depression." *Archives of General Psychiatry* 55: 1128–32.

Moore, Thomas J. 1989a. *Heart Failure: A Critical inquiry into American Medicine and the Revolution in Heart Care.* New York: Random House.

————. 1989b. "The Cholesterol Myth." *Atlantic Monthly* 264 (3) (September): 37–70.

————. 1993. *Lifespan: Who Lives Longer and Why.* New York: Simon and Schuster.

Morgan Stanley Dean Witter. 1998. "The New R&D Paradigm: an Investor Guide—The Midas Principle."

Morrison, Steven A., and Clifford Winston. 1995. *The Evolution of the Airline Industry.* Washington, D.C.: Brookings Institution.

National Bipartisan Commission on the Future of Medicare. 1999. "Final Breaux-Thomas Medicare Reform Proposal." Washington, D.C.

National Institutes of Health, National Heart, Lung, and Blood Institute. 1997. *The Sixth Report of the Joint National Committee on Prevention, Detection, Evaluation, and Treatment of High Blood Pressure.* NIH publication 998-4090.

————. 1998. *Clinical Guidelines on the Identification, Evaluation, and Treatment of Overweight and Obesity in Adults: The Evidence Report.*

————. National Cholesterol Education Program. 1993. "Second Report of the Expert Panel on Detection, Evaluation, and Treatment of High Blood Cholesterol in Adults (Adult Treatment Panel II)." NIH Publication 93-3096.

References

—————, National Institute of Neurological Disorders and Stroke. 1998. "New Stroke Treatment Likely to Decrease Health Care Costs and Increase Quality of Life." Press release.

Nemeroff, Charles B. 1998. "The Neurobiology of Depression." *Scientific American,* June.

Nordenberg, Tamar. 1998. "It's Quittin' Time: Smokers Need Not Rely on Willpower Alone." *FDA Consumer,* February. www.fda.gov.

Office of the President, National Economic Council, Domestic Policy Council. 1999. "Disturbing Truths and Dangerous Trends: The Facts about Medicare Beneficiaries and Prescription Drug Coverage."

Organisation for Economic Co-operation and Development. 1999. *OECD Health Data 1999.* Washington, D.C.: OECD.

Pauly, Mark. 1999. "Can Beneficiaries Help Save Medicare? Beneficiary Contributions and Medicare Reform." In *Medicare in the Twenty-first Century: Seeking Fair and Efficient Reform,* edited by Robert B. Helms. Washington, D.C.: AEI Press.

Peltzman, Sam. 1973. "An Evaluation of Consumer Protection Legislation: The 1962 Drug Amendments." *Journal of Political Economy* 81 (September–October):1049–91.

—————. 1987. "The Health Effects of Mandatory Prescription Regulation." *Journal of Law and Economics* 30 (2)(October):207–38.

Peterson, Walter L., and Cryer, Byron. 1999. "COX-1-Sparing NSAIDs: Is the Enthusiasm Justified?" *Journal of the American Medical Association* 282 (20) (November 24): 1961–63.

Peveler, Robert, Charles George, Ann-Louise Kinmonth, Michael Campbell, and Chris Thompson. 1999. "Effect of Antidepressant Drug Counselling and Information Leaflets on Adherence to Drug Treatment in Primary Care: Randomized Controlled Trial." *British Medical Journal* 319 (September 4): 612–15.

Pharmaceutical Research and Manufacturers of America. 1999. *Pharmaceutical Industry Profile.* Washington, D.C.: PhRMA.

Pitt, Bertram, David Waters, William Virgil Brown, Ad J. Van Boven, Leonard Schwartz, Lawrence M. Title, Daniel Eisenberg, Linda Shurzinske, and Lisa S. McCormick. 1999. "Aggressive Lipid-Lowering Therapy Compared with Angioplasty in Stable Coronary Artery Disease." *New England Journal of Medicine* 341 (2) (July 8): 70–76.

Preston, John, John H. O'Neal, and Mary C. Talaga. 1994. *Handbook of Clinical Psychopharmacology for Therapists.* Oakland, Calif.: New Harbringer Publications.

Ramsay, Lawrence E., Bryan Williams, G. Dennis Johnston, Graham A. MacGregor, Lucilla Poston, John F. Potter, Neil R. Poulter, and Gavin Russell. 1999. "British Hypertension Society Guidelines for Hypertension Management 1999: Summary." *British Medical Journal* 319 (September 4): 630–35.

Reissman, Debi. 1998. "Issues in Drug Benefit Management: Back to Compliance." *Drug Benefit Trends* 10 (10): 18.

References

Richmond, Mark H. 1999. *Human Genomics: Prospects for Health Care and Public Policy.* London: Pharmaceutical Partners for Better Healthcare.

Ross, Susan D., I. Elaine Allen, Janet E. Connelly, Bonnie M. Korenblat, M. Eugene Smith, Daren Bishop, and Don Luo. 1999. "Clinical Outcomes in Statin Treatment Trials." *Archives of Internal Medicine* 159 (August 9–23):11793–801.

Schwartz, Lisa, and Steven Woloshin. 1999. "Finding and Redefining Disease." *Effective Clinical Practice* 2 (2) (April): 76–86.

Secondary and Tertiary Prevention of Stroke Patient Outcome Team. 1996. *Ninth Progress Report.*

Serdula, Mary K., Ali H. Mokdad, David F. Williamson, Deborah A. Galuska, James M. Mendlein, and Gregory W. Heath. 1999. "Prevalence of Attempting Weight Loss and Strategies for Controlling Weight." *Journal of the American Medical Association* 282 (14) (October 13):1353–58.

Shephard, James, Stuart M. Cobbe, Ian Ford, Christopher G. Isles, A. Ross Lorimer, Peter W. Macfarlane, James H. McKillop, and Christopher J. Packard. 1995. "Prevention of Coronary Heart Disease with Pravastatin in Men with Hypercholesterolemia." *New England Journal of Medicine* 333 (20) (November 16).

Showstack, J., et al. 1989. "The Effect of Cyclosporine on the Use of Hospital Resources for Kidney Transplantation." *New England Journal of Medicine* 321 (16).

Simon, Lee S., Arthur L. Weaver, David Y. Graham, Alan J. Kivitz, Peter E. Lipski, Richard C. Hubbard, Peter C. Isakson, Kenneth M. Verburg, Shawn S. Yu, William W. Zhao, and G. Steven Geis. 1999. "Anti-inflammatory and Upper Gastrointestinal Effects of Celecoxib in Rheumatoid Arthritis: A Randomized Controlled Trial." *Journal of the American Medical Association* 282 (20) (November 24):1921–28.

Simoons, M. L., and A. F. Casparie. 1999. "Treatment and Prevention of Coronary Heart Disease by Lowering Serum Cholesterol Concentration: Third Consensus Cholesterol." Report to the Netherlands government.

"The SOLVD Investigators." *New England Journal of Medicine* 325 (5): 293–302.

Teitelbaum, Fred, Andrew Parker, Ruth Martinez, and Catherine Roe. 1999. *Express Scripts Drug Trends Report, 1998.* Maryland Heights, Mo.: Express Scripts.

Thomas, Lacy Glen. 1994a. "Pricing, Regulation, and Competitiveness—Lessons for the U.S. from the Japanese Pharmaceutical Industry." *Pharmacoeconomics* 6 (supp. 1): 67–70.

————. 1994b. "Implicit Industrial Policy: The Triumph of Britain and Failure of France in Global Pharmaceuticals." *Industrial and Corporate Changes* 3 (2): 451–90.

Thompson, David, John Edelsberg, Graham A. Colditz, Amy P. Bird, and Gerry Oster. 1999. "Lifetime Health and Economic Consequences of Obesity." *Archives of Internal Medicine* 159 (18) (October 11): 2177–83.

References

Tierney, John. 1998. "At the Intersection of Supply and Demand." *New York Times Magazine,* May 4.

Triplett, Jack, ed. 1999. *Measuring the Prices of Medical Treatments.* Washington, D.C.: Brookings Institution.

Tufts Center for the Study of Drug Development. 1999. "Clinical Development Times for New Drugs Drop 18%, Reversing 12-Year Trend." *Impact Report* (July).

——————. 1999. "European and U.S. Approval Times for New Drugs Are Virtually Identical." *Impact Report* (November).

U.S. Department of Health and Human Services, Health Care Financing Administration. 1999. "National Health Care Expenditures by Type of Service and Source of Funds: Calendar Years 1960–1997." Washington, D.C.: Government Printing Office.

——————. 1999. Conversation with AEI staff. December 30.

U.S. Government Accounting Office. 1999. Testimony of Laura A. Dummit before the Subcommittee on Health and Environment, Committee on Commerce, House of Representatives, September 28. Washington, D.C.: GAO.

Vakil, Nimish. 1996. "Guidelines for H. pylori-Induced Peptic Ulcer Disease Treatment." *Drug Benefit Trends* 8 (B): 21–24, 32.

Williamson, David F. 1999. "Pharmacotherapy for Obesity." *Journal of the American Medical Association* 281 (3) (January 20): 278–80.

About the Author

John E. Calfee is a resident scholar at the American Enterprise Institute. During 1980–1986, he served in the Bureau of Economics at the Federal Trade Commission. He later taught in the business schools of the University of Maryland at College Park and Boston University.

Mr. Calfee has written numerous scholarly articles and opinion pieces on advertising, health, tort liability, and other topics. He is the author of *Fear of Persuasion* (1997).